图书在版编目（ＣＩＰ）数据

永恒的面孔：古埃及的黄金木乃伊 / 深圳市南山博
物馆编. -- 北京：文物出版社，2022.5
ISBN 978-7-5010-7369-6

Ⅰ．①永… Ⅱ．①深… Ⅲ．①干尸－埃及－古代－通
俗读物 Ⅳ．①K884.118.8-49

中国版本图书馆CIP数据核字(2022)第047322号

THE FACE OF ETERNAL LIFE
Egypt and Its Golden Mummies

永恒的面孔
古埃及的黄金木乃伊

编　　者：深圳市南山博物馆

责任编辑：智　朴

责任印制：张　丽

出版发行：文物出版社

社　　址：北京市东直门内北小街 2 号楼

网　　址：http://www.wenwu.com

经　　销：新华书店

印　　制：雅昌文化（集团）有限公司

开　　本：889mm × 1194mm　1/16

印　　张：16.25

版　　次：2022 年 5 月第 1 版

印　　次：2022 年 5 月第 1 次印刷

书　　号：ISBN 978-7-5010-7369-6

定　　价：420.00 元

主办单位	**ORGANIZER**
深圳市南山区文化广电旅游体育局	Shenzhen Nanshan District Administration of Culture, Radio, Television, Tourism and Sports

承办单位	**HOST MUSEUM**
深圳市南山博物馆	Nanshan Museum

参展单位	**LOAN INSTITUTIONS**
英国曼彻斯特博物馆	Manchester Museum
诺玛德展览有限公司	NOMAD EXHIBITIONS (UK) Limited

策展人	**CURATOR**
坎贝尔 · 普赖斯	Campbell Price

展览组织与实施	**EXHIBITION ORGANIZATION AND IMPLEMENTATION**

深圳市南山博物馆	**Nanshan Museum**
总策划：戚　鑫	General Planning: Qi Xin
展览策划：刘　昉	General Coordination: Liu Fang
展览统筹：黄海滨	Exhibition Curation: Huang Haibin
展览执行：郭岱伦	Exhibition Coordination: Guo Dailun
展陈设计：方丹霞　陈思敏　林洁纯　冯　时	Exhibition Design: Fang Danxia, Chen Simin, Lin Jiechun, Feng Shi
宣传推广：刘佳妮　余秀清　李怡婵　刘晏鑫	Communication: Liu Jiani, Yu Xiuqing, Li Yichan, Liu Yanxin
社会教育：张亚东　陈梓仪　白之仑　邱　烨	Exhibition Publicity & Public Education: Zhang Yadong, Chen Ziyi, Bai Zhilun, Qiu Ye
展品管理：方楚瑜　郑　宇	Conservation: Fang Chuyu, Zheng Yu
展览协助：王　钒	Exhibition Assistance: Wang Fan
展览摄影：曾耀乐	Photography: Zeng Yaole

目录 CONTENTS

序言
PREFACE

    木乃伊、黄金和对来世的迷恋——这些观念都是我们对"古埃及"印象的核心构成。这些观念对于埃及人来说有多重要呢?它们在最后一位法老之后又影响了埃及多久?本次展览探讨了在埃及历史上相对不为人所熟知的"希腊-罗马"时期（公元前 300~ 公元 300 年）的埃及人对来世的期望。这一历史时期始于一个希腊的王国——马其顿王国对埃及的统治，在托勒密王朝的女王克里奥帕特拉七世后，罗马的君主控制了埃及。

    这个多元文化社会中的富有群体为来世做了精心的准备，结合了埃及、希腊和罗马关于永恒之美的理想。曼彻斯特博物馆隶属于英国曼彻斯特大学，是除了开罗以外最好的古埃及文物收藏地之一。这些藏品是在 19 世纪 80 年代至 20 世纪 10 年代英国统治埃及期间发掘出来的，我们对这些文物的观察和理解更多是基于我们今天的视角，而不是当时制造和使用它们的人的视角。

Mummies, gold and an obsessive belief in the afterlife – these concepts are all central to our image of 'Ancient Egypt'. But how important were they to the Egyptians, and how long did they survive after the last of the Pharaohs? This exhibition explores expectations of a life after death during the relatively little-known 'Graeco-Roman' Period of Egyptian history – when Egypt was ruled first by a Greek royal family, ending with Queen Cleopatra VII, then by Roman emperors (between 300 BC and AD 300).

Wealthy members of this multicultural society made elaborate preparations for the afterlife, combining Egyptian, Greek, and Roman ideals of eternal beauty. Manchester Museum, part of the University of Manchester in the United Kingdom, houses one of the finest collections of this material outside Cairo. Excavated during a time of British rule of Egypt in the 1880s–1910s, our responses to these objects may reveal more about ourselves than about the people who made and used them.

坎贝尔·普赖斯博士

DR. CAMPBELL PRICE

坎贝尔·普赖斯博士自 2011 年以来一直担任曼彻斯特博物馆古埃及和苏丹分馆馆长。曼彻斯特博物馆是英国最大的古埃及文物藏馆之一。普赖斯在利物浦大学完成了埃及学的学士、硕士和博士学位，目前任该校荣誉研究员。他曾在埃及塞加拉和开罗的埃及博物馆从事田野考古工作。

坎贝尔发表了大量关于古埃及物质文化的文章，并对博物馆里"古埃及"的雕塑和建筑一直有着特殊的研究兴趣。最新著作有《口袋里的博物馆：古埃及》（2018）和《埃及黄金木乃伊——解读"希腊 - 罗马"时期的特征》（2020）。他多次参加相关国际会议并发表演讲，经常在电视和广播媒体上就埃及学主题发表评论和建议。

2021 年，坎贝尔被任命为埃及探索协会理事长，该协会是支持和促进埃及文化遗产保护最重要的慈善机构之一。

Dr Campbell Price has been Curator of Ancient Egypt and Sudan at the Manchester Museum, one of the UK's largest Egyptology collections, since 2011. He completed his BA, MA, and PhD in Egyptology at the University of Liverpool, where he is now an Honorary Research Fellow. Campbell has undertaken fieldwork in Egypt at the sites of Zawiyet Umm el-Rakham, Saqqara and the Egyptian Museum, Cairo.

Campbell has published widely on ancient Egyptian material culture and maintains special research interests in sculpture and the construction of 'Ancient Egypt' in museums. Recent books include *Pocket Museum: Ancient Egypt (2018)* and *Golden Mummies of Egypt: Interpreting Identities from the Graeco-Roman Period (2020)*. He has lectured internationally, and regularly comments and advises on Egyptological themes for TV and radio.

In 2021, Campbell was appointed Chairman of Trustees at the Egypt Exploration Society, one of the foremost charities supporting and promoting Egyptian cultural heritage.

坎贝尔·普赖斯博士 DR. CAMPBELL PRICE

埃及黄金木乃伊

希腊、罗马与埃及的世界在法老时代的末期发生了碰撞。数百件闪闪发光的金器、绘画与木乃伊被葬入墓中。

大约 2000 年后，埃及工人在哈瓦拉遗址发现了一片巨大的墓区。现在，曼彻斯特博物馆将通过一场全新的巡回展览审视这些非同寻常的考古发现。

19 世纪 80 年代，英国考古学家威廉•马修•弗林德斯•皮特里（1853 ~ 1942 年）雇佣了一支由数百名埃及工人组成的考古队，对法尤姆绿洲入口附近的哈瓦拉遗址进行发掘。虽然最初吸引他前来此处的是第十二王朝法老阿蒙涅姆赫特三世（约公元前 1831~ 前 1786 年）的金字塔和与金字塔建筑群有关的传说中的"迷宫"，但最终促使他留在这片遗址继续进行考古活动的却是此间出土的大量"希腊 - 罗马"时期的文物。皮特里对这些（部分）文物充满热情——在埃及历史上，"希腊 - 罗马"时期是文物最为丰富的时代。但颇具讽刺意味的是，这也是最为人所忽视的历史时期之一。

杰西•霍沃斯（1835 ~ 1920 年），曼彻斯特的"棉花大王"，同时也是积极的反教阶制基督徒。在霍沃斯的资助下，皮特里实现了发掘"迷宫"的雄心。他本以为能够找到中王国时期的墓葬，最终却发现了大批"希腊 - 罗马"时期的文物，以至于无法（也可能是不愿）对大多数物品，尤其是墓葬进行准确的记录。他偏爱饰有醒目彩绘画像的木乃伊——这种艺术风格源自意大利，他认为这是埋葬在法尤姆的人来自希腊或罗马的直接证明。

皮特里对饰有镀金石膏面具的木乃伊评价不高，他曾在日志中抱怨，"镀金木乃伊还在继续'泛滥'"，并称之为"这些带着镀金面具和彩绘头像的可怜东西"。

在工人挖出的所有木乃伊中，带装饰的"希腊 - 罗马"时期木乃伊仅占 2% 左右；大多数都是未经装饰的"普通"木乃伊，皮特里在处理这些木乃伊时干净利落、残忍无情。他声称："至于那些没有画像也没有棺木的可怜的木乃伊，我们每天都会一打一打地搬过来。"他对制作和埋葬木乃伊的人的态度大相径庭。

木乃伊面具
托勒密时期（公元前 332 年～公元前 30 年）
拉罕金字塔，法尤姆地区
（曼彻斯特博物馆，藏品编号 2120）
摄影：朱莉娅•索恩

这件面具脸部镀金，饰以绘有卷发和辫子的三翼头饰（或假发），前额垂有刘海。这些证据表明这张面具是为女性而制，展现了逝者希望在来世所拥有的接近神明的理想样貌。头饰的流苏末端绘有奥西里斯等冥界之神。

熠熠之躯

在法老时代，埃及人认为死亡是一种分解：人会被分解成不同的部分。丧葬仪式的目的是将这些部分重新组合起来，并使结成的整体能够获得永生。从新王国时期一直到后王国时期，埃及人对于逝者的三重影响范围有着一套基本的表述：

"巴灵翱翔于天际，

尸体暂存于阴间，

雕像供奉在寺庙。"

（埃及开罗博物馆第 3 号纸草）

男性木乃伊
罗马时期的埃及
法尤姆绿洲
（曼彻斯特博物馆，藏品编号 1767）
摄影：迈克尔 · 波拉德

这幅彩绘画像镶嵌在一张覆盖在罗马时期木乃伊上半身的石膏面具中；画中男子有着深色卷发、络腮胡和浅色八字胡。从画像的相貌与发型来判断，这幅画的创作时间约为哈德良统治时期（约公元117 ～ 138 年）。

在"希腊 - 罗马"时期，"巴"的流动性通常是一切葬礼经文的重点。巴被刻画为人首鸟身的形象，出现在墓葬装饰、《亡灵书》和后来的随葬品或葬仪用品中。

至少从这个角度来看，保住肉身是永生的先决条件。木乃伊仪式的目的是创造一个适合永生的逝者形象——在埃及文献中被称为"Sah"（灵体）。虽然有时会被简单地翻译成"木乃伊"，但这个术语的含义和关联却要复杂得多。

从图像学上来说，"Sah"通常表现为某种不规则的、被遮蔽的形状，通过遮盖肢体，弱化被裹成蛹状的部位的人类特征。它强调的是大量亚麻布的包裹，以及增强被包裹的物体身上的神圣力量。被布条包裹的人体通常戴着长长的三叠头罩——多为蓝色，以代表与众神相似的青金石色头发。

这种神圣的包裹物通常被称为"人形"棺和木乃伊面具，比如这里所展示的这件女性木乃伊盖板，埃及学文献常称其为"木乃伊棺"。事实上，更恰当的说法是木乃伊模仿了这种神化的"Sah"的形态，而不是"Sah"被描绘成了木

木乃伊面具

托勒密时期

哈瓦拉，法尤姆绿洲

（曼彻斯特博物馆，藏品编号 2178a）

摄影：朱莉娅·索恩

　　这张面具饰有的蓝色假发，让人联想到众神的青金石发色，面具头戴一个由莲花花蕾和花朵组成的花环，象征着新生命的希望。

女性木乃伊盖板

罗马时期的埃及

科普托斯城，上埃及

（曼彻斯特博物馆，藏品编号 1763）

摄影：朱莉娅·索恩

　　这是一副女性木乃伊盖板。她的脸部、脖子和裸露的胸部全都是镀金的，发型是长且黑的螺旋形长卷发，头戴红色花环。这种精致的发型强调了性在重生中的重要性，并将这名女子与哈托尔女神和伊希斯女神联系在一起。

乃伊的模样。"人形棺"和"木乃伊棺"这类术语也具有误导性:"人形"通常用于描述被遮盖住的"Sah"的形态——实际上包裹处理的目的是让尸体更像是神化的"Sah"而不是人。

诠释特征

皮特里对"希腊-罗马"时期"粗旷"的葬礼装饰风格极为不满,认为导致铭文混乱的原因是外来文化的影响和知识的匮乏;这种批评的声音至今依然存在。根据皮特里的说法,"当时,象形文字已被人遗忘,铭文部分或是模糊不清,或是空白一片。"事实上,象形文字显然对罗马人有着巨大的吸引力,这有助于在某些情况下将这种文字保存下来,否则它可能在更早的时候就已被废弃不用。

撇开象形文字的质量,曼彻斯特博物馆的一些藏品体现了与各类木乃伊盖板及棺木相关的画像主题所具有的价值。根据墓葬风格和铭文判断,这具名为塔希里安克的年轻女性的木乃伊棺显然来自阿赫米姆。该遗址位于卢克索以北约 100 公里处,中世纪时因神庙遗迹而闻名,直到 19 世纪仍是一处著名景点。

19 世纪 80 年代,阿赫米姆的墓葬数量之多令法国发掘者应接不暇。大多数美观的文物被他们出售,只有少数送至开罗的布拉奇博物馆进行登记,其他(可能是无装饰的)木乃伊则被卖给造纸厂,或是最终成为埃及铁路的燃料!

塔希里安克和她的棺木正是通过这种方式流入蒙茅斯郡议员乔治·艾略特爵士(George Elliot, 1814～1893 年)手中。他曾任埃及总督财政顾问,鼓励英国首相本杰明·迪斯雷利(Benjamin Disraeli)投资苏伊士运河。这样的交易无疑为他提供了获得古董——至少是两具木乃伊的机会,两具木乃伊均被认定为"公主"。艾略特在惠特比有一处住所,据说哥特恐怖作家布莱姆·斯托克(Bram Stoker)曾去过那里——说不定塔希里安克是斯托克于 1903 年出版的小说《七星宝石》的灵感来源。

棺木和木乃伊盖板上的名字"塔希里安克"让我们确信,她确实是这具棺材预定的主人,但事实并非总是如此。她的名字在埃及语中的意思是"活着的(女)孩",这或许反映出在婴儿死亡率居高不下的时代,她出生时父母的喜悦之情。她的父亲名叫伊雷托里

塔希里安克木乃伊棺
托勒密早期(约公元前 300 年)
阿赫米姆,上埃及
(曼彻斯特博物馆,藏品编号 13783)
摄影:朱莉娅·索恩

塔希里安克的棺木上饰有一张镀金面具(绘有明亮而富有表情的双眼)和涂成蓝色的三叠假发。

对木乃伊进行的 CT 扫描显示,塔希里安克的主要器官已被摘除,被分别包裹之后重新放回体内。

X 光显示,塔希里安克死亡时大约 20 岁。(大约是在托勒密时代的早期,这是根据面具上的那双大眼睛,以及对其的称呼是"哈托尔"而非"奥西里斯"来进行推断的。)

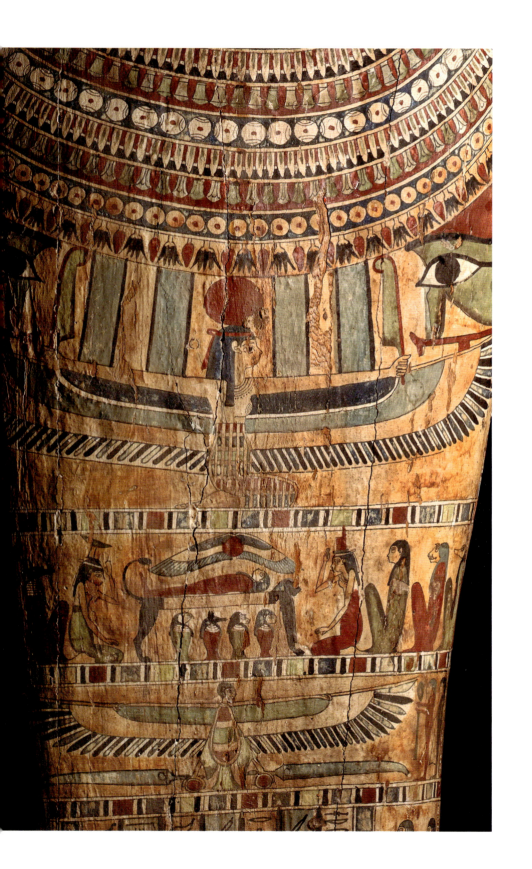

塔希里安克木棺盖细部图

托勒密早期（约公元前 300 年）

阿赫米姆，上埃及

（曼彻斯特博物馆，藏品编号 13783）

摄影：朱莉娅·索恩

　　塔希里安克的木棺盖板上绘有覆盖羽
毛的神像（也许是努特），以及在有翼
太阳盘下的木乃伊化的奥西里斯——代表
着黎明时分升起的太阳。这一场景将塔
希里安克与每日重生的象征联系在一起。

鲁 （意为"荷鲁斯正瞪着他们"，即一个人的敌人）。他是阿赫米姆最重要的神灵"敏"的祭司；她的母亲叫穆特霍特普 （意为［女神］穆特很满意"），她是"敏"的摇铃人。父母的头衔都证实了盖板装饰风格与"敏"的崇拜中心阿赫米姆有着千丝万缕的联系。在节选自《亡灵书》的铭文中，逝者被称作"哈托尔·塔希里安克" 。这是将女性逝者与西方女神哈托尔而非奥西里斯联系在一起的最早的例证之一。

塔希里安克的棺木显示，她是一个变形的"Sah"，头戴代表神性的蓝色头罩；丰腴的身姿和相对较大的眼睛都是当时阿赫米姆的许多木乃伊棺的典型特征，其他各个装饰元素也是如此。

与"希腊-罗马"时期随葬画像中的许多元素一样，"伸展翅膀的女神"这一主题至少可以追溯到第 21 王朝棺木上大量出现的画像——也许还要更早。人们认为这位无处不在的女神可能是伊希斯、哈托尔、玛特或努特。努特的可能性最大，因为她是早期棺木中最常援引的神灵。

女神下方是一段重要的简介，概括了将尸体有效转化为"Sah"的过程。它展现了躺在狮形棺上的木乃伊，两侧是伊希斯和奈芙蒂斯。这两位女神曾奇迹般地帮助兄弟奥西里斯实现了重生。狮形床是托勒密时代晚期象形文字中的一个标记，念作"mki" ，意为"保护"——这说明每幅图中图标隐含了多重意义。

棺下方的卡诺皮克罐是虚构的；托勒密时期已不再使用实体罐，CT 扫描显示，塔希里安克的内脏在被包裹好之后已放回胸腔之中。

将逝者的某些部分直接与指定的神明联系起来，可以进一步确保其获得神的保护。与阿赫米姆出土的另一些托勒密时代的木乃伊棺一样，塔希里安克的木棺中也有《亡灵书》第 42 章的一组经文——一段对抗杀戮者的咒语。这段经文以逝者的口吻，宣布自己身体的所有部分均与神灵有所关联，经文以一句提示结束：

"我的身体里处处有神明。"

虽然这种"图像盔甲"将逝者置于神力的护佑之中，但它也宣称逝者本身具有神性。可以说，对塔希里安克身为"哈托尔"所具有的神性最简单的"陈述"，就是木棺上的镀金面具。

寻找黄金

在哈瓦拉出土的"希腊-罗马"时期的上层阶级墓葬中，最引人注目的一个特点是以大量黄金装饰木乃伊。从巴哈利亚绿洲 (Bahariya Oasis) 等当代墓地（contemporary cemeteries）可以看出，殡葬业中的炫耀性黄金消费似乎在"希腊-罗马"时期尤为典型。

为了减少黄金脱落的风险，除镀金的木乃伊棺和面具外，一些木乃伊的外层绷带上也贴了金箔；舌头、手指和眼睛上覆盖着金色的饰物，镀金的部分直接粘在肌肤上。一些木乃伊画像头顶的花环与双唇之间也添加了金箔。

金箔的自由使用是逝者家庭财富的一个明显指标，并有着一些相当具体的宗教含义。经典神话故事《天牛之书》(Book of The Celestial Cow)暗指众神拥有金色的身体，新王国后期的一些皇家墓室证实了这一点。人们经常引用《天牛之书》来证明制作神像的理想材料是黄金，事实上它描绘的是一个神处于"半封印"状态下，缺乏力量的表现。即便由最为稳定和持久的材料构成，神在世间的肉体也很容易受到攻击，需要物理和仪式上的防御。

给遗体镀金可以增强和肯定逝者的神性，也许这种做法与将逝者与太阳结合在一起的专门仪式有关。"希腊 - 罗马"时期埃德富和丹德拉神庙的经文中明确记述了这种将神像搬上神庙屋顶，让它们在阳光直射下"重新吸收能量"的仪式。

在《亡灵书》第154章"防止尸体消亡"咒语的一些晚期版本中，展示了躺在棺木上，接受阳光照射的木乃伊。这与更早期的概念相关，并对其有所延伸；例如，对第三中间时期"黄色棺木"这一独特颜色的一种解释是，它们代表了太阳神"拉"发出的光（并在某种意义上将光线反射回"拉"那里）。公元 1 世纪的一篇经文——即所谓的"防腐仪式"，简明扼要地描述了黄金在这方面所具有的神力：

"愿他（拉）在阴间照亮你的脸，

你以黄金呼吸，

你乘着黄金前行。"

（公元 1 世纪的防腐仪式）

哈瓦拉的镀金女性木乃伊

在阿赫米姆的塔希里安克的木乃伊棺上发现的基本图像元素也出现在 1911 年皮特里在哈瓦拉发掘的一具公元 1 世纪的女性木乃伊的外裹尸布上。这位女士相当不寻常，根据木乃伊面具顶部用希腊字母标识的名字，她很可能是"德米特里奥斯的女儿伊索斯（或伊萨欧斯）"（Isaious [or Isarous] daughter of Demetrios）。

木乃伊面具

托勒密时期

出处未知

（曼彻斯特博物馆，藏品编号 6286）

摄影：朱莉娅·索恩

这张微笑的面具被置于一具木乃伊的头上。脸部的镀金区域由矩形金箔贴成，其他部分的皮肤则被涂成黄色。面具的下颌处还有两个标记，可能是模仿更早的"胡须带"（beard straps）或中王国时期一些木乃伊面具上的项链。

伊索斯女性木乃伊棺

"希腊－罗马"时期

哈瓦拉，法尤姆绿洲

（曼彻斯特博物馆，藏品编号 11630）

摄影：迈克尔·波拉德

　　这件木乃伊的上半身覆盖着镀金的面具，说明逝者是一位被理想化的"希腊－罗马"时期女性。

伊索斯的装饰足盒

"希腊－罗马"时期

哈瓦拉，法尤姆绿洲

（曼彻斯特博物馆，藏品编号 11630）

摄影：迈克尔·波拉德

　　这些借自法老时代的样式化"外国人"代表了"逝者敌人"这一普遍概念。这种足盒也许可以使木乃伊在下葬前能够直立摆放一段时间。

木乃伊的上半身覆盖着精致的镀金面具:姑娘手持花环，有着一头精致的大波浪和额前排列紧密的螺旋状卷发，饱满的脸庞让人想起了托勒密王朝时期的理想容貌。面具饰有大量珠宝，包括镶有半宝石的项链和蛇形手镯，在法老时代，这种手镯可以利用蛇所具有的保护力量。由此，面具给人留下了"这是一位罗马贵妇理想化的样貌"的印象，显示出那些在童年夭折的人对来世享受成年生活的期望。

伊索斯的木乃伊上还有大量传统的法老时代的意象（traditional Pharaonic iconography）。面具的背面和下部，或比较靠下的部分（目前被包裹物遮盖）都有传统的埃及图案。在染了红色颜料的外裹尸布上挂着一个宽大的衣领。其下，努特跪在代表黄金的象形文字符号上展开双翼，两侧是阿努比斯和托特。再下面，豺首人身的阿努比斯再次出现，照料着棺木上逝者的木乃伊——配有罗马时期已不再使用的罐子。最后是一个褪色相当严重的奠酒场景;在这个场景以及尸体两侧的场景中，这位已故的女士完全以传统的法老时代的形象出现。场景标题中的象形文字几乎都是可读懂的，绝非皮特里所说的"大错特错"。这表明在同一个墓葬中可能会使用不同的表现形式和风格。

"希腊 - 罗马"时期覆盖面具的木乃伊和肖像木乃伊都配有模制"足盒"，展示了裹尸布中露出的穿着凉鞋的脚。脚下绘有被缚的敌人，喻义其永被践于脚底。这些人实际上是死者的仇人，而不是普通的"囚犯"，这一点在一些足盒的标题中有明确的表述:"鞋下的敌人"——这是对早期神庙中一个短语的改编，这个短语通常和神与法老的互动场景一起出现。

在"希腊 - 罗马"时期，"踩在脚下的敌人"可能还代表了一种更普遍的隐喻:战胜死亡，获得永久的安宁。雕塑和彩绘画像木乃伊均使用了足盒等元素，这表明埃及人对逝者有着普遍的潜在期望。学术界和流行术语中，"画像"（反映了相似性）和面具（隐藏或改变身份的手段）之间的传统对立掩盖了这种密切的联系。

这是对早期神庙中一个短语的改编，这个短语通常和神与法老的互动场景一起出现。

此文章在 《尼罗河》 杂志第 24 期 （2020 年 3-4 月刊） 第一次发表。

女孩木乃伊

罗马时期的埃及

哈瓦拉，法尤姆绿洲

（曼彻斯特博物馆，藏品编号 1769）

摄影：朱莉娅·索恩

　　这名年轻女性的面具正面是镀金的，面具上的罗马发型可以追溯到公元 1 世纪中期。

　　女孩在来世重生时看起来非常漂亮：她的面具反映了当时的时尚，包括镶嵌玻璃的珠宝和蛇形手镯。木乃伊的脚上套着露趾足盒——可能是为了炫耀她漂亮的凉鞋。

GOLDEN MUMMIES OF EGYPT

Towards the end of the age of the pharaohs, the Greek, Roman and Egyptian worlds collided. Hundreds of glittering gold objects, paintings and mummies, were buried.

Some 2,000 years later, Egyptian workers discovered a vast necropolis at the site of Hawara. Now, a new travelling exhibition from Manchester Museum examines these extraordinary discoveries.

In the 1880s, British archaeologist William Matthew Flinders Petrie (1853-1942) employed a team of hundreds of Egyptian workers to excavate the Egyptian site of Hawara. Although he was initially attracted by the Twelfth Dynasty pyramid of King Amenemhat III (c. 1831-1786 BCE) and the lure of the legendary 'Labyrinth' that once formed its associated temple complex, Petrie stayed at the site because of the vast quantity of material from the Graeco-Roman Period. Despite's Petrie's eventual enthusiasm for (some of) its remains, this period of Egypt's history is – ironically – both its most object-rich yet also one of its most overlooked.

Due to financial sponsorship from Manchester cotton magnate – and active non-conformist Christian – Jesse Haworth (1835-1920), Petrie was able to realise his ambition of digging at the site of the 'Labyrinth'. Expecting to find Middle Kingdom tombs, Petrie was so overwhelmed with the quantity of Graeco-Roman finds that it was impossible – and perhaps undesirable – to make an accurate record of the majority of objects, especially burials. He favoured mummies with striking painted panel portraits attached – a stylistic import from Italy – which he came to prize as direct evidence of the Greek or Roman identity of people living and dying in the Faiyum.

Petrie was less complimentary about mummies with gilded, moulded plaster masks, complaining in his diary that 'the plague of gilt mummies continues', 'wretched things with gilt faces and painted head pieces'.

Mummies of Graeco-Roman date with any form of decoration made up only around two per cent of those Petrie's workers' excavated; the majority being undecorated - 'plain' – specimens, and Petrie was ruthlessly efficient in working through these, claiming: 'as for poor mummies without painting or

CARTONNAGE MUMMY MASK
PTOLEMAIC PERIOD (332–30 b.c.)
EL-LAHUN, FAIYUM
MANCHESTER MUSEUM, ACC. NO. 2120
PHOTO: JULIA THORNE

This mask has a gilded face and a tripartite headdress or wig, painted to represent curls and plaits, with a fringe over the forehead.
This suggests that the mask was made for a woman. It shows her in the idealized, almost divine form that the dead hoped to have in the afterlife. At the ends of the headdress lappets, some of the gods of the dead are depicted, including Osiris.

cases, we heave them over by the dozen every day.' How different were his attitudes to the people who made and buried the mummies.

Scintillating Flesh

Death in Pharaonic Egypt was conceptualised as a dismemberment, the breaking up of a person into their constituent parts. Funerary ritual aimed at reuniting these parts and making the re-formed whole durable for eternity. A basic formulation of the three spheres of influence of the deceased occurs from the New Kingdom until the Late Period:

Your Ba shall endure in the sky,

your corpse in the Underworld,

your statues in the temples.

(Papyrus Boulaq III *, Egyptian Museum, Cairo)*

During the Graeco-Roman Period, it is the mobility of the Ba that is generally the focus of funerary texts of any length. The Ba was visually conceptualised as a human-headed bird in vignettes of the Book of the Dead or excerpts from it that appear in tomb decoration, later funerary compositions or other funerary objects.

Survival of the body was, at least from this standpoint, a prerequisite for eternal life. The aim of the ritual of mummification was to create an image of the deceased fit for eternity – what is referred to in Egyptian texts as a 'Sah'. Although sometimes translated simply as 'mummy', the meanings and associations of the term are more complex.

Iconographically, the *Sah* ⌠ typically took a somewhat amorphous, shrouded shape that deemphasised the human-ness of the form enclosed – chrysalis-like – within by obscuring individual limbs. Instead, emphasis was placed both on conspicuous

This painted portrait is set into a plaster mask which covers the upper body of a Roman-era mummy; it depicts a man with dark curly hair, a full beard, and a light mustache. The appear ance and hairstyle of the portrait suggests a date sometime around the reign of Hadrian, ca. a.d. 117–138.

GILDED CARTONNAGE MUMMY COVER

ROMAN EGYPT
KOPTOS, UPPER EGYPT
MANCHESTER MUSEUM. ACC. NO. 1763
PHOTO: JULIA THORNE

This mummy cover for a woman. The woman's face, neck, and bare breasts are gilded. Her hair is arranged in long, dark corkscrew curls, and she wears a wreath of red flowers on top of her head. This elaborate hairstyle emphasises sexuality in the service of rebirth and connects the woman to the goddesses Hathor and Isis.

This mask features a blue wig, reminiscent of the lapis lazuli hair of the gods, and a wreath of lotus buds and blossoms around the head, symbolising the promise of new life.

consumption of linen and the power of the cloth to maintain and amplify the sacredness of the hidden object underneath. This wrapped figure usually wears a long, tripartite head-covering – most often coloured blue, to represent the lapis lazuli hair associated with physical manifestations of the gods.

Such a shrouded divine form is commonly referenced by 'anthropoid' coffins and mummy masks and is often referred to as 'mummiform' in Egyptological literature; in fact, it is probably more appropriate to speak of the mummy emulating this divinised Sah form than gods being depicted in the shape of mummies. Coffin terminology is also misleading: 'anthropoid' is regularly used to describe the shrouded Sah form – intended to be more divine than human in shape.

Reading representations

Petrie was highly critical of the 'crude' style of Graeco-Roman funerary decoration, dismissing garbled inscriptions as due to foreign influence and lack of knowledge; such pejorative assessments persist today. For Petrie, writing about material from the Roman Period, 'hieroglyphs were by then forgotten, inscribed parts being all fudge or blanks.' In fact, hieroglyphic script clearly held a fascination for the Romans, and this helped sustain the script in certain contexts where otherwise it might have become obsolete much sooner.

Irrespective of the quality of the hieroglyphs, the value of the iconographic themes pertaining to a broad range of mummy covers and coffins can be illustrated through some examples now in Manchester Museum.Based on its style and inscriptions, the coffined mummy of a young woman named Tasheriankh – formerly identified as 'Salford II' – clearly derives originally from Akhmim. The site, about 100km north of Luxor, was renowned in the Medieval period for its standing temple remains described by Arab travellers, and remained a noted attraction into the Nineteenth Century.

The quantity of material at Akhmim overwhelmed French excavators in the 1880s; most aesthetically-pleasing items were offered for sale and only a small number of items were registered at the Boulaq Museum in Cairo, with (presumably undecorated) mummies being sold to paper manufacturers or ended up as fuel for the Egyptian railways.

It is from this source that Tasheriankh and her coffin entered the possession of Sir George Elliot (1814-1893), Member of Parliament for Monmouthshire, who also acted as a financial adviser to the Egyptian

Khedive and encouraged British Prime Minister Benjamin Disraeli to invest in the Suez Canal. Such dealings would no doubt have afforded the opportunity to acquire antiquities, notably at least two mummies which each became identified as a 'Princess'. Elliot maintained a residence at Whitby, where he is known to have been visited by the gothic horror writer Bram Stoker; perhaps, therefore, Tasheriankh was the inspiration for Stoker's 1903 novel 'The Jewel of Seven Stars'.

Tasheriankh's name – repeated several times on her coffin and mummy cover – assures us that she is indeed the intended occupant of the coffin, which is not always the case. Her name means literally 'the living (female) child', a reflection perhaps of an exclamation of joy at her birth in the context of high infant mortality rates. Her father is named Irethoriru ⟨hieroglyphs⟩ (lit. 'the eye of Horus is against them (i.e. one's enemies)' and he was a priest of Min, the preeminent god of Akhmim; her mother was a sistrum-player of Min called Muthotep ⟨hieroglyphs⟩ (lit. '(the goddess) Mut is satisfied'). Both parents' titles confirm the stylistic association with Akhmim, the cult-centre of the god Min. The deceased is referred to in the inscriptions – excerpts of the Book of the Dead – as the 'Hathor Tasheriankh' ⟨hieroglyphs⟩, one of the earliest cases of identifying the female deceased with the goddess of the west rather than with Osiris.

Tasheriankh's coffin shows her as a transfigured Sah with the blue-coloured head-covering of divinity; its particular voluminousness and the relatively large eyes are both typical of many coffins of the period from Akhmim – as are the individual decorative elements.

Like many elements in Graeco-Roman funerary iconography, the common motif of a goddess with outstretched wings can be traced back at least to the iconographic explosion on coffins of the Twenty-first Dynasty if not even earlier. The identity of this ubiquitous goddess has been variously suggested as Isis, Hathor, Maat, or Nut. The latter seems most likely, as Nut is the deity invoked most frequently on earlier coffins.

Beneath the goddess is a key vignette showing the mummy on a lion-form bier flanked by Isis and Nephthys, the goddesses who effect the rebirth of their brother Osiris. The lion-form bed appears in the hieroglyphic script of the Late and Ptolemaic Period as a sign read 'mki' ⟨hieroglyph⟩ – 'protection' – illustrating the multiple layers of potential iconographic meaning encoded in each vignette. The

inclusion of canopic jars beneath the bier is a fiction; provision of physical jars had fallen out of use by the Ptolemaic Period and CT-scans show that Tasheriankh's wrapped internal organs have been returned to the chest cavity.

Further divine protection was secured by identifying parts of the deceased directly with named deities. In common with a number of other Ptolemaic coffins from Akhmim, Tasheriankh was provided with a panel of text from Chapter 42 of the Book of the Dead – a spell against slaughterers. The text is voiced from the perspective of the deceased declaring divine associations with each body part and ends with a rubric that states:

'there is no body-part of mine devoid of a god'.

While this iconographical armour encased the deceased with divine protection, it also asserted the divinity of the deceased themselves. Arguably the simplest statement of Tasheriankh's divinity – as a 'Hathor' – is the gilded face of her coffin.

Going for gold

One of the most notable features of the elite burials of Graeco-Roman Hawara was the large amount of gold used to decorate mummies. Attested from contemporary cemeteries such as at Bahariya Oasis, such conspicuous consumption of gold in the funerary industry does seem particularly typical of Graeco-Roman times.

To reduce the risk of detachment, in addition to gilded coffins and masks, gold leaf was applied to the outer bandages of some mummies; gold covers were placed on the tongue, fingers and eyes, and gilding was also adhered in sections directly to the flesh. On some portraits panels it is also to be noted that gilding was added to depictions of garlands worn in the hair and between the lips.

An apparent indicator of the wealth of the family of the deceased, the liberal use of gold leaf had several rather specific religious meanings. The classic mythological narrative which alludes to the gods having golden flesh is the '*Book of the Celestial Cow*', attested from a number of royal burial chambers in the later New Kingdom. Although the text is often quoted to demonstrate the ideal

Tasheriankh's coffin has a gilded face (with large, expressive eyes) and a tripartite wig, painted blue. CT scans of her mummy reveal that Tasheriankh's major organs had been removed, separately wrapped, and then replaced within the body. X-rays indicate that Tasheriankh was around 20 when she died, probably in the early Ptolemaic Period, judging by those large eyes on her mask, and the fact that Tasheriankh is referred to as "Hathor", rather than Osiris.

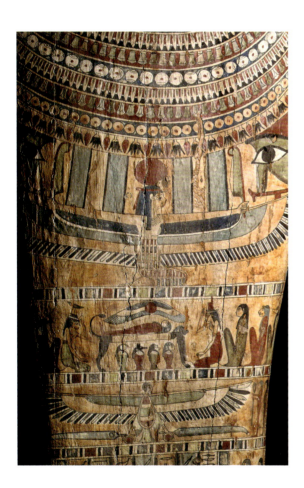

Tasheriankh's coffin lid features a feathered figure of (probably) Nut, and a mummified Osiris beneath a winged sun disc, representing the rising sun at dawn. The scene connects Tasheriankh with this symbol of daily rebirth.

materials from which to craft divine cult statues, it in fact depicts a sub-par manifestation of the god, in a compromised state – semi-fossilised, not at full strength. Even if composed of apparently enduring and untarnishable materials, the gods' physical bodies on earth were susceptible to attack and required physical and ritual defences.

Gilding the corpse promoted and affirmed the divinity of the deceased, but is perhaps specifically to be linked to the rite of uniting the deceased with the sun. This ritual, of taking statues of the gods onto the temple roof to 'recharge' them in direct sunlight, is articulated explicitly in texts at the Graeco-Roman temples of Edfu and Dendera.

A vignette of some late versions of Book of the Dead Chapter 154, the "Spell for not letting a corpse perish", shows the mummy laid on a bier, with the sun's rays streaming down upon it. This correlates with and extends earlier concepts; for example, one interpretation of the distinctive colouring of Third Intermediate Period " yellow coffins" is that they represent sunlight emanating from (and in some sense reflected back to) the sun god Re. A 1st century a.d. text, the so-called "Embalming Ritual", succinctly describes the divine power of gold in this context:

"May he (Re) illuminate your face in the underworld,

You breathe by gold,

and you go forth by gold."

(Embalming Ritual, from the 1st century AD.)

A gilded lady from Hawara

The same basic iconographic components found on the coffin of Tasheriankh from Akhmim were applied directly to the outer shroud of a First Century CE female mummy from Petrie's 1911 excavations at Hawara. The lady is – rather unusually – identified by name in Greek letters at the top of her cartonnage mask. Initially interpreted as 'Demetria, wife of Icaious' this is more likely to be a patronymic: Isaious (or Isarous) daughter of Demetrios (Ἰσαιοῦς/Ἰσαροῦς Δημη[τρίου]).

The upper part of the mummy is covered by an elaborate mask modelled in cartonnage and gilded, showing the deceased holding a wreath, with

This smiling mask was to be placed over the head of a wrapped mummy. The gilding on the face was applied using rectangles of gold leaf, while the rest of the skin is painted yellowish-tan. The mask also sports two markings on the chin which may emulate either much earlier 'beard straps' or parts of necklaces that appear on some Middle Kingdom mummy masks.

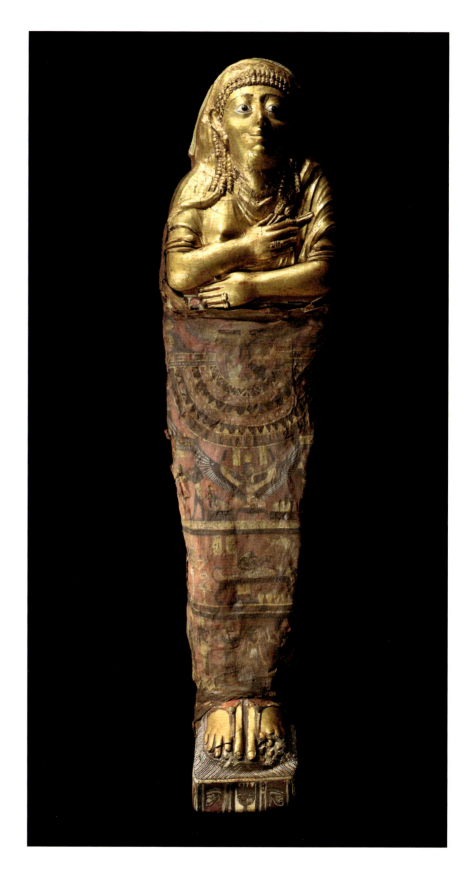

CARTONNAGE MUMMY MASK OF ISAIOUS

GRAECO-ROMAN PERIOD
HAWARA, FAIYUM OASIS
MANCHESTER MUSEUM, ACC. NO. 11630
PHOTO: MICHAEL POLLARD

The upper part of the mummy of lady Isaious is covered with
a gilded cartonnage mask showing the deceased as an idealised
Graeco-Roman woman.

elaborate coiffure of lightly waved hair and tight corkscrew curls, and full face reminiscent of some Ptolemaic ideals. The rich jewellery comprises necklaces set with semi-precious stones and snake bracelets of the sort that harnessed the serpent's protective power from Pharaonic contexts. The resulting impression is of the idealised appearance of a Roman lady of high status. The same iconography is shared by another gilded mummy of a small girl from Hawara, showing the expectation of a full adult existence in the afterlife for those who had died as children.

Isaious is also provided with a rich panoply of traditional Pharaonic iconography. On the back and underside of the cartonnage mask or on lower sections (presently obscured by wrappings), are traditional Egyptian motifs. On the outer, mainly red-pigmented shroud, hangs a broad (*wesekh*) collar. Under this, Nut kneels on the hieroglyphic symbol for gold and extends her wings flanked by scenes of the gods Anubis and Thoth. Beneath, the jackal-headed Anubis appears again tending the mummy of the deceased on a bier – equipped with canopic jars that no one would have used in the Roman Period. Finally, a rather faded libation scene appears; in this and in the scenes that flank the sides of the body, the deceased lady is shown in entirely traditional Pharaonic mode and, far from being 'blundered' (in Petrie's expression), the hieroglyphs in the captions to the scenes are almost all readable. This shows the range of possible representations and styles that might be used in a single funerary composition.

Common to both masked and portrait mummies of the Graeco-Roman Period are moulded cartonnage footcases showing the sandal-shod feet emerging from the wrappings. On the underside – and thus eternally trampled – are depictions of bound enemies on the soles of the feet. That these are in fact the enemies of the deceased and not generic 'prisoners' is stated explicitly by captions in some examples - 'your enemies under your sandals' - an adaptation of a standard phrase that accompanies depicted interactions between gods and the Pharaoh in earlier temples.

In Graeco-Roman times, the trampled enemies may represent a more general metaphor of triumph over death and the resulting attainment of eternal peace. The fact that elements such as footcases appear on both the sculpted and painted-faced mummies points towards a common underlying expectation for the deceased. The traditional opposition in scholarly and popular terminology between 'portrait' (a revealing likeness) and a mask (a means of concealing or altering the identity) obscures this close connection.

DECORATED FOOTCASE OF ISAIOUS

GRAECO ROMAN PERIOD
HAWARA, FAIYUM OASIS
MANCHESTER MUSEUM. ACC. NO. 11630
PHOTO: MICHAEL POLLARD

These stylised 'foreigners' borrow from Pharaonic iconography to represent the generic idea of the enemies of the deceased. Such footcases may have enabled the mummy to be stood upright for a period before burial.

This article was first published in NILE Magazine,

issue #24, March–April 2020.

WRAPPED MUMMY OF A YOUNG GIRL

ROMAN EGYPT
HAWARA, FAIYUM OASIS
MANCHESTER MUSEUM, ACC. NO. 1769
PHOTO: JULIA THORNE

The front of this young girl's mask is gilded and shows the deceased with a type of Roman hairstyle which can be dated to the mid-1st century a.d. This girl was reborn in the afterlife looking her very best: her mask depicts the fashion of the day, and includes jewellery inlaid with glass, and snake-shaped bracelets. A cartonnage footcase fits over the wrapped feet of her mummy, the toes of which are shown peeking out—probably to show off her fine sandals.

瓦拉采石场")指这个建筑是石料的来源，从而为今天它几乎完全损毁提供了一个颇为可信的解释。

皮特里在哈瓦拉

皮特里应该对那些讲述迷宫故事的古希腊典籍极为熟稔，他也知道以前有很多人在哈瓦拉挖掘文物。这些因素至少一定程度上促使他在下一次向埃及文物局申请发掘许可时，选择哈瓦拉为工作地点。他的发掘工作揭开了哈瓦拉许多不为人知的秘密，这些令人惊叹的发现让这个遗址声名鹊起。到 1896 年，哈瓦拉的名气已经如日中天，以至于古典主义者大卫·G·贺加斯（David G. Hogarth）开始叹息："一定是因为它无与伦比，它的信徒才不厌其烦地谈论所谓埃及学，就好像世上没有其他考古学，而且在埃及的发现给予再多的盛赞之辞也不为过。在尼罗河上的薄雾笼罩之下，迈锡尼、尼尼微和庞贝被人遗忘。探险家极力吹捧哈瓦拉或代赫舒尔，他们认为这些地方是一个逝去的时代美轮美奂的重现。"[8]

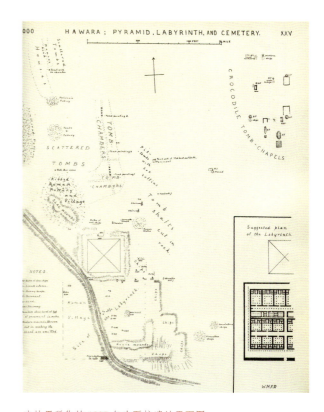

在关于 1888 年第一次在哈瓦拉进行考古发掘的公开记录中，皮特里开篇就提到，法国人尤金·格雷波（Eugène Grébaud）已经"决定将法尤姆省划给我；当时没有任何人在那里发掘过——文物部门已经有 25 年没有涉足过那里。"格雷波曾在 1886～1892 年间担任埃及文物局的负责人。

皮特里的这段描述在掩饰他一直觊觎哈瓦拉这一事实。他的朋友，埃及探险基金创始人阿米莉亚·爱德华兹（Amelia Edwards）在 1887 年 1 月 19 日写给皮特里的一封信中提及，曼彻斯特实业家杰西·霍沃斯（Jesse Haworth）"是那种可能愿意发掘'迷宫'的人"。最后，正是在霍沃斯的支持之下，许多重要的哈瓦拉文物被收入曼彻斯特大学曼彻斯特博物馆的藏品之中。

1888 年 1 月，皮特里在哈瓦拉开始动工。英国或埃及政府没有给予支持，他对此耿耿于怀，在发掘报告中尖锐地指出，"目前的考察只是私人事业，由两位朋友杰西·霍沃斯先生和马丁·肯纳德（Martyn Kennard）先生鼎力支持。他们两位挺身而出，承担了大部分费用。"

皮特里显然对（新近确立的）发掘文物分配制度也有所不满。他抱怨说，埃及政府"把我找到的大部分东西拿走了，放到埃及博物馆，以作为我获得发掘许可的代价。那个博物馆要真是个安全的地方也就

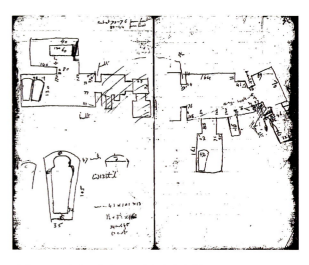

皮特里日记中哈瓦拉晚王国时期陵墓的草图

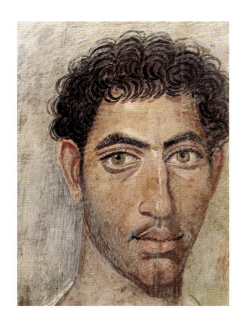

出土于哈瓦拉的青年彩绘木乃伊画像，制作于
公元 2 世纪
（曼彻斯特博物馆，藏品编号 2263）

出土于哈瓦拉的成年女性彩绘木乃伊画像，
制作于公元 2 世纪
（曼彻斯特博物馆，藏品编号 2266）

罢了。"[9] 皮特里将他在哈瓦拉的发掘成果中的很大一部分运送到国外。

　　毫无疑问，皮特里被传说中的迷宫吸引到哈瓦拉，他的主要任务是探究阿蒙涅姆赫特金字塔内部的秘密，确定陵墓王室主人的身份，并发掘那些令人赞叹的晚王国时期竖井墓，但是对金字塔周围"希腊 - 罗马"时期墓区的发掘占用了他大部分的时间和资源。用他自己的话说，"虽然我为金字塔而来，但我很快在彩绘木乃伊画像中发现了一座宝矿。"[10]

　　古希腊罗马时期墓区（大部分位于金字塔北部）的考古发现情境（archaeological context）并没有被皮特里妥善地记录下来。借助皮特里对其发现有限的细节描述，我们可以大致还原他发现木乃伊时这些墓区的情形。[11] 解释哈瓦拉遗址的一个主要障碍是，木乃伊存放位置的建筑可能重新利用了之前被采石活动损毁的建筑（主要是泥砖）。所以即便皮特里做了任何地层学研究的详细记录——往好的方面说——也是非常棘手。事实上皮特里在埃及考古中根本没有使用地层学方法，只在巴勒斯坦使用了。

"骷髅头随波漂荡"

　　皮特里的笔记中提到了与当地村民保持一定距离的好处，最好避开跟随他们的那些"游手好闲的人"，在发掘现场附近扎营。[12] 皮特里在写给英国国内资助人的信中画了一幅草图，给与帐篷相邻的一个区域标上"头骨室"字样，那里保存着人类遗骸——特别是从有彩绘画像的木乃伊上取下来的有趣的头骨。在皮特里笔记的其他地方，他将这个区域描述为"我那些木乃伊朋友的停尸间"，声称"我住所的木乃伊多得难以处理"[13]，皮特里回忆说，"重要的木乃伊就放在我的床下"。来访的赞助人马丁·肯纳德的随侍对生活在"一群木乃伊"当中感到厌恶不已。[14]

　　根据皮特里的描述，他在哈瓦拉的发掘工作可算是他更为大胆的冒险之一。尤其是他对 1888～1889 年间清理晚王国时期墓葬过程的回忆，依稀可以看出他可能就是《夺宝奇兵》里印第安纳·琼斯的原型。哈瓦拉的一些墓穴竖井很深，一直通向地下墓室，那里的墓葬依然完整，不过因为地下水位较高，里面的有机物大部分已遭到破坏。

　　皮特里在一具石棺的两侧发现两个隐藏的隔间，每个隔间里都有大量的乌夏勃梯雕像，它们是逝者的替身或仆人。当工人告诉他发现了"像蜡烛一样大的画像"时，皮特里非常激动，迅速赶到现场。他回忆道，从竖井进入坟墓的过程如同"坠入地狱"，为了方便起见，他不得不脱掉衣服，跳入地下墓室的脏水中。这里的水恶心不堪，皮特里只能将头伸出水面，并试图用脚移动乌夏勃梯，"此时骷髅头随波漂荡"。[15]

特里在1891年给一位赞助者的信中称，"一具普通木乃伊需要5英镑；10英镑可以买一具漂亮的木乃伊。"[29]

甚至在1888年秋天，也就是他在哈瓦拉的第二个季节，皮特里谈到"阿拉伯商人法拉克"在那里的发现"许多常见的镀金面具，那些我都不屑一顾。"[30]他声称，到1911年，他不得不在现场留下"许多镀金半身像木乃伊"，因为它们"大部分已经腐烂得无法移动"。[31]

对于那些"无处不在"的镀金墓葬装饰，皮特里心里多少有些厌恶，但他当然知道他在英国北部的朋友对纺织品的热情及其在这个方面的宝贵专业知识。1888年4月，他从哈瓦拉写信给阿奎拉·道奇森牧师："请告诉你的好朋友布拉德伯里先生，如果他愿意，希望他能查检所有带图案的布料。如果能得到一份技术报告，我将感激不尽"。[32]

那套最好的哈瓦拉纺织物"都经过浸泡、清洗和熨烫"，打包后送往曼彻斯特，[33]一批有代表性的纺织物送往博尔顿和谢菲尔德等其他英国工业中心。皮特里没有指明大多数"纺织物"的来源，但它们肯定几乎全部来自木乃伊的包裹物。

皮特里考古事业的赞助商并不认为向纺织业人士公开展示这些样本而造成了任何价值损失，相反它们进一步激发了他对考古工作的热情。1912年，棉花大王杰西·霍沃斯在曼彻斯特埃及和东方协会的一次会议上，向众人展示了皮特里1887～1889年在哈瓦拉发掘出来的一批亚麻纺织品，明确指出它们与现代英国纺织业的联系，并将这些"非凡的布匹"比作"现在每周在兰开夏郡生产出来的布匹"[34]。当时的埃及棉直接供应英格兰西北部的纺织厂，并为熟悉纺织业的人士提供了一个独特的视角，以审视那些古代成就。

抢救与阐释

与埃及其他遗址一样，数百名埃及男子、妇女和儿童承担了哈瓦拉及其他遗址的许多工作，但他们很少在出版物中被提及。[35]该国的殖民基础设施也促成了英国人的考古挖掘。皮特里在其发掘报告中向英国官员、法尤姆省公共工程督察休特（Hewat）少校致谢，感谢他"在我逐步处理木乃伊和文物的同时，允许

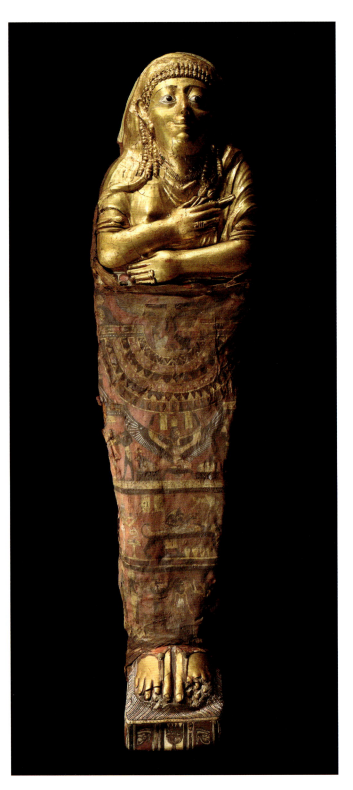

出土于哈瓦拉的一位名叫伊索斯的女性的木乃伊，制作于公元1世纪，有彩绘木乃伊棺和镀金石膏

（曼彻斯特博物馆，藏品编号11630）

出土于哈瓦拉的彩绘木乃伊胸部盖板残片，属于托勒密王朝时期一名叫尼玛特的男性
（曼彻斯特博物馆，藏品编号2112）

每周更多的木乃伊和文物涌进来，堆放在（少校的）办公室里。"[36]——这是一个重要的暗示，说明英国对这个国家的委任统治权使他有可能得到后勤支持。皮特里在他的写作过程中，将殖民机器带来的西方式秩序和专业知识与工人的情绪化、焦虑和普遍的不信任进行对比；[37]小费成为"激励考古发现"的手段。[38]他的叙述包含着一种内在的矛盾。他鄙视一种交易关系，却支持另一种交易关系。

尽管皮特里表现出对工作的一丝不苟、有条不紊，但他自己在遗址中却选择性地抢救木乃伊，只对那些能产生收益的木乃伊估价："我打开数十个竖井墓穴，但只有一个能不亏本。"[39]带有装饰的"希腊-罗马"时期木乃伊仅占发掘出来的木乃伊的百分之二左右，[40]大部分都未经装饰，是"普通"的木乃伊，皮特里在处理这些木乃伊时干净利落、残忍无情。他声称："至于那些没有画像也没有棺木的可怜的木乃伊，我们每天都会一打一打地搬过来。"[41]

而对于那些认为值得保存的木乃伊，皮特里尝试了各种保存技术——特别是在脆弱的表面涂上石蜡，以起到加固作用，并"修复一些画像的暗沉区域"。[42]在1911年的一张照片中，一些木乃伊上面的画像被报纸遮住，以防烈日暴晒。据说有些木乃伊在运送到英国的途中被陈列在甲板上，在太阳底下晒干。[43]皮特里认为从一些木乃伊身上取下画像，从而避免它们在运输过程中受损是一种好办法。[44]当两者都到达博物馆时，再将画像放回到在保存完好的木乃伊棺中。[45]

皮特里的田野考古在英国和其他地方广为人知，这很大程度上是因为他为了筹集资金，不遗余力地提高自己的知名度。他精心挑选一年一度的考古文物展的地点和时间；1888年

6～7月，这次他没有如往常一样，选择伦敦牛津大厦作为展览场地，而是将哈瓦拉出土的文物放在伦敦皮卡迪利区埃及大厅附近的剧院中展出，并提前对严肃媒体开放数场"撩人"的预展——参观者有东方主义画家劳伦斯·阿尔玛·达德玛（Lawrence Alma-Tadema），或许还有作家奥斯卡·王尔德（Oscar Wilde），他的中篇小说《道林·格雷的画像》可能从法尤姆肖像中那位令人难忘的英俊少年身上获得了灵感。[46] 皮特里向阿米莉亚·爱德华兹报告这次展览时说："虽然那天的天气很恶劣，但展厅里一切进展顺利……我预计一个人能大约赞助100英磅……这比我预期的要好……几个可靠的人来过了……都不只来了一次。我们找的是同道中人，绝对不要那种恶心粗俗的人参加。"[47]

此类发掘成果展览，以及媒体对他们的报道，巩固了皮特里作为"英雄考古学家"的声誉，人们赞扬他为英国带来许多珍贵文物。他精力充沛，凡事亲力亲为——比如在考古现场露营、探索危险的地下墓穴和发掘那些不可思议的宝藏等等。这些在他自己对哈瓦拉那段时间的日志里最为详尽。毫无疑问，一直到20世纪，这些都持续着影响大众对考古工作的认知。

然而，皮特里本人显然不像他在日志中经常暗示的那样独自行动，大部分"发现"也不是他作出的；他雇用的众多埃及工人只是在他自己的叙述中偶然出现，他们常常因为一些缺点或闹情绪而受到责备。他对自己的发现成果表现出明显的偏见——从那以后，他的看法在"希腊-罗马"时期文物的埃及学评价中，不断激起回响。

皮特里利用与某些英国官员的关系以及整个殖民机器（尤其是分配制度）将文物输送给西方如饥似渴的公众。因此，在萨克斯·儒默（Sax Rohmer）前三部非常东方化的傅满洲小说（1913～1917年）中，那位对抗邪恶东方大反派的英国中坚人物的名字叫"皮特里博士"，也就毫不奇怪了。[48]

出土于哈瓦拉的罗马时期玻璃容器
（曼彻斯特博物馆，藏品编号 2068）

|注释|

本文是《黄金木乃伊——彩绘面具》（Golden Mummies, Painted Faces）一书第一章的节略版，该书将作为曼彻斯特博物馆"希腊-罗马"时期墓葬文物的哈瓦拉文物国际巡展的衍生品出现。埃及黄金木乃伊展于2020年2月8日在纽约布法罗科学博物馆开幕。

1. M. Lehner, The Complete Pyramids (1997, London), 181-183.

2. 关于金字塔群后来可能重建的情况，请参见 E. P. Uphill, Pharaoh's Gateway to Eternity: the Hawara labyrinth of King Amenemhat III. Studies in Egyptology. (2000, London & New York).

3. 关于"希腊-罗马"时期哈瓦拉地区对阿蒙涅姆赫特三世的崇拜，以及对该遗址的全面考察，请参见 I. Uytterhoeven, Hawara in the Graeco-Roman period: life and death in a Fayum village. Orientalia Lovaniensia Analecta 174 (2009, Leuven), 423-448.

4. 《历史》第二卷148；参见 D. Asheri, A.B. Lloyd and A., Corcella, A Commentary on Herodotus Books I-IV (2007, Cambridge), 348-350. for commentary, with conjectural reconstruction of structure described in Herodotus, Pliny and Strabo.

5. 这方面的经典研究参见 A. B. Lloyd, "The Egyptian Labyrinth," Journal of Egyptian Archaeology 56,(1970) 81-100. 另见 Uytterhoeven，238-247.

6. 参见 C. Malleson, The Fayum Landscape. Ten Thousand Years of Archaeology, Texts and Traditions in Egypt (2019, Cairo), 147-187, within the wider context of perceptions of the Faiyum.

7. Uytterhoeven, 1.

8. D. G. Hogarth, A Wandering Scholar in the Levant (1896, London), 171-2.

9. W. M. Flinders Petrie, Hawara, Biahmu and Arsinoe (1889, London), 3-4.

10. 在皮特里自传中，有许多关于此类展览的夸张描述：W. M. Flinders Petrie, Seventy Years in Archaeology (1931, London), 83.

11. Uytterhoeven, 183-237; P. C. Roberts. "An archaeological context for British discoveries of mummy portraits in the Fayum"，见 J. Picton, S. Quirke 和 P. C. Roberts 主编的 Living Images: Egyptian funerary portraits in the Petrie Museum, 13-57 (Walnut Creek, CA),13-57。

12. Petrie, 1889, 3.

13. Roberts 2007, 23.

14. 对这一事件的热烈讨论参见 Petrie，1931年，82。

15. W. M. Flinders Petrie, Kahun, Gurob and Hawara (1890, London), 9.

16. 同上，9。

17. 关于霍鲁贾的乌夏勃梯，参见 G. Janes, The Shabti Collections 5: A Selection from the Manchester Museum (2012, Cheshire), 392-434。关于根据哈瓦拉考古发现建立的霍鲁贾家谱，参见 Uytterhoeven，511-512。

18. 例如 Petrie, 1890, 8-11.

19. 参见皮特里1888年1月22-29日的日记：Roberts, 84.

20. 希罗多德（历史 II, 148)) 也提到过，鳄鱼木乃伊在皮特里发掘的"希腊-罗马"时期人类坟墓的底部：Petrie, 1889, 17.

21. 同上，Petrie, 14-21.

22. 类似的小型玻璃容器在巴哈利亚绿洲出土的同期木乃伊中也有出现，参见 Z. Hawass, The Valley of the Golden Mummies (2000, New York), 73.

23. 关于皮特里的叙述，参见 Petrie, 1889, 14-17。

24. 皮特里1888年3月4日的日记：Roberts, 94。皮特里在其自传中使用了同样的措辞：Petrie, 1931, 88.

25. 皮特里1888年3月的日记：Roberts 2007, 39。

26. 同上，96.

27. B. Moon. '"A Fearful Outbreak of Egyptology' in the North West"（在 ASTENE 会议上宣读，2005, Manchester, 未发表），6.

28. 关于一直被忽视的开罗博物馆销售部门的运作，参见 P. Piacentini, "The antiquities path: from the Sale Room of the

Egyptian Museum in Cairo, through dealers, to private and public collections.A work in progress" (2013-14, Milan, Egyptian & Egyptological Documents, Archives, Libraries 4), 105-130。

29. H. Forrest. Manufacturers, mummies and Manchester: two hundred years of interest in and study of Egyptology in the greater Manchester area. BAR British Series 532 (2011, Oxford), 27.

30. 皮特里 1888 年 10 月的日记：Roberts, 23。

31. 皮特里 1911 年 2 月 26 日的日记：Roberts and Quirke, 104。

32. Moon 2005, 3

33. Petrie 1889, 4: "采用合理的技术将最重要、最完整的一套将被送到曼彻斯特博物馆。"

34. W.M. Crompton, "Report of the Manchester Egyptian and Oriental Society, 1913," Journal of the Manchester Egyptian and Oriental Society 2, 12.

35. 关于这些"看不见的手"，参见 S. Quirke, Hidden hands: Egyptian workforces in Petrie excavation archives 1880-1924. Duckworth Egyptology (2010, London:).

36. Petrie, 1889, 4.

37. 例如，"当地人对待这个遗址都比较粗暴，不在乎这些砖的脱落"（Petrie, 1890, 6）；据说在哈瓦拉盗窃陵墓的行为很普遍（Petrie 1931, 90）。

38. Petrie ,1889, 3.

39. 同上 , 8.

40. Uytterhoeven, 22 和 58。

41. 皮特里 1888 年 1 月 29 日到 2 月 5 日的日记：P.C.Roberts 和 S. Quirke，参见 J. Picton, Janet 主编的 "Extracts from the Petrie Journals"。

S. 参见 Quirke 和 P. C. Roberts 主编的 Living Images: Egyptian funerary portraits in the Petrie Museum (2007,Walnut Creek, CA), 83-104。

42. Petrie, 1889, 19.

43. Petrie, 1931, 89.

44. Roberts, 29.

45. 同上 , 87.

46. D. Montserrat, "Unidentified human remains: mummies and the erotics of biography" in D. Montserrat, ed., Changing bodies, changing meanings: studies on the human body in antiquity (1998, London & New York), 162-197.

47. 1888 年 7 月 12 日皮特里致爱德华兹的信。

48. 参见 R. Luckhurst, The Mummy's Curse: the true history of a dark fantasy (2012, Oxford), 168-9。

FLINDERS PETRIE (AND OTHERS) AT HAWARA

Amenemhat III (Reigned ca. 1842-1797 BC)

William Matthew Flinders Petrie (1853-1942) (Internet photo)

British-born William Matthew Flinders Petrie (1853-1942) was arguably the most prolific archaeological fieldworker operating in Egypt during the last two centuries. He was active – directing a large number of Egyptian workers – at a huge number of sites but one that held a special place for him was that of Hawara. Although praised as the 'Father of Egyptian Archaeology', Petrie's methods and attitudes deserve being revisited in order to better understand the context and interpretation of his finds.

The site of Hawara is located on the southern edge of the Faiyum region, a fertile depression about 80km south of modern-day Cairo. Dominated by the pyramid built by the Twelfth Dynasty King Amenemhat III (c. 1831-1786 BC), the site's importance was no doubt instigated by this ruler. Only the mud-brick core of Amenemhat's pyramid now survives but the finished edifice once rose to around 58 metres in height and was clad in gleaming white limestone, resembling the great pyramids of the Old Kingdom. Amenemhat's pyramid stood – in a rather unusual arrangement for the time – to the north of a major rectangular enclosure (some 385 by 158 metres),[1] which forms the largest pyramid complex from the Middle Kingdom and the last major example of such in Egyptian history.

In design Amenemhat's Hawara complex appears to have been modelled on the Step Pyramid complex of the Third Dynasty King Djoser (c. 2667-2648 BC) at Saqqara, the first monumental edifice ever realised in stone to such proportions. Together, Djoser and Amenemhat III bookend a millennium of such ambitious pyramid construction in Egypt. Amenemhat built a first pyramid at Dahshur but by his 15th regnal year began construction of a second complex at Hawara, known as 'Ankh-Amenemhat' ('May Amenemhat live') if quarrying inscriptions at Wadi Hammamat are to be positively linked with the site; these mention statues destined for the establishment, of which there were likely to have been many at the Hawara complex, although now poorly attested.[2]

While the royal pyramid was intended to be sealed after the king's burial, the adjoining 'mortuary' temple was designed to be an eternal hub of activity, focussed on celebrating a perpetual cult for the deceased pharaoh. In this

Mud-brick core of the ruined Pyramid of Amenemhat III at Hawara. (Internet photo)

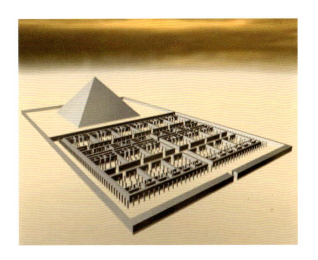

Computer-generated re-construction of the Pyramid of
Amenemhat III & adjoining funerary temple

aim, the Hawara complex was particularly effective – because Amenemhat III is one of rather few pharaohs to have received continuing worship as a god long after his death. A good indication of the ongoing veneration of the king is the number of people named after him even into Roman times.[3] Thus, in the Late Period some men were named 'Nimaatre' after his prenomen – or throne name. Indeed the prominent cult of the deified Amenemhat III during the Graeco-Roman Period in various Faiyum towns some distance from Hawara may have prompted people to be buried next to the Labyrinth/pyramid. We may note, for example, the stated desire of an unknown man who made his will at Tebtunis, some 20km south-west of Hawara, in the reign of Hadrian (117-138 AD), to be buried 'near the Labyrinth'.

Karl Lepsius's sketch of the ruins at Hawara in the 1840s, from his Denkmäler aus Ägypten und Äthiopien (Berlin, 1849).

The afterlife of Amenemhat's pyramid complex

The afterlife of Amenemhat's pyramid complex is, however, even more remarkable than that of the king himself. Several Greek and Roman sources in the last centuries BC and first centuries AD – the period in which Hawara functioned as a major cemetery – identified the structure with the Classical Labyrinth, based on a comparison with the legendary maze designed by Daedalus for King Minos at Knossos in Crete. Writing in the Fifth Century BC, Herodotus[4]provides a singular description of the site – especially notable considering the fact that he hardly mentions Theban monuments, which appear so memorable to modern visitors to Egypt. Herodotus attributed the construction of the Labyrinth to twelve kings rather than Amenemhat III alone, and it is worth quoting his description extensively:

'I visited this place, and found it to surpass description; for if all the walls and other great works of the Greeks could be put together in one, they would not equal, either for labour or expense, this Labyrinth… The Labyrinth surpasses the pyramids. It has twelve courts, all of them roofed, with gates exactly opposite each other, six looking to the north, six looking to the south. A single wall surrounds the entire building. There are two different sorts of chambers throughout – half under ground, half above ground, the latter built upon the former; the whole number of these chambers is three thousand, fifteen hundred of each kind. The upper chambers I myself passed through and saw, and what I say concerning them is from my own observation; of the underground chambers I can only speak from report: for the keepers of the building could not be got to show them, since they contained (as they said) the sepulchres of the kings who built the Labyrinth, and also those of the sacred crocodiles… [the upper chambers] excel all other human productions; for the passages through the houses, and the varied windings of the paths across the courts, excited in me infinite admiration, as I passed from courts into chambers, and from chambers into colonnades, and from colonnades into fresh houses, and from these again into courts unseen before. The roof throughout was of stone, like the walls; and the walls were carved all over with figures; every court was surrounded by a colonnade, which was built of white stones, exquisitely fitted together. At the corner of the Labyrinth stands a pyramid, forty fathoms high, with large figures engraved upon it; which is entered by a subterranean passage.'

Further bombast and perplexity – some of it no doubt derivative of Herodotus – appears in accounts written by various Greek and Latin authors: Diodorus Siculus, Strabo, Pliny the Elder, Pomponius Mela, Manetho and Eusebias.[5]The Labyrinth also featured on the itineraries of

Fanciful plan of the Labyrinth by Athanasius Kircher (1602-1680).

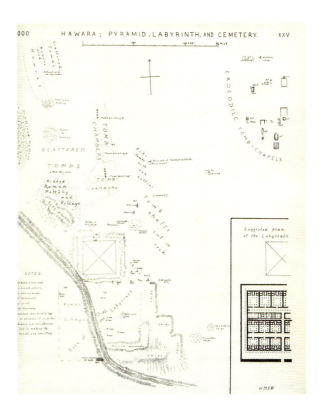

Petrie's 1889 plan of the site of Hawara.

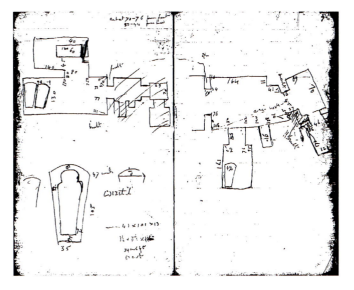

Petrie's sketch of Late Period tombs at Hawara, from his journal.

the Roman senator Lucius Memmius, who visited the Faiyum region in 112 BC, and three centuries later by the Emperor Septimius Severus, 199-200 AD. In each account, the use of the word 'Labyrinth' conveys some sense of the magnitude and complexity of the structure to a Greek audience and the allure of the Labyrinth persistently overshadows any other features of the landscape in subsequent accounts. Although the Faiyum landscape is described by a number of Arabic writers in Medieval times, none make specific mention of Hawara or the Labyrinth.[6]

The first encounter of modern West and the Labyrinth

Recorded modern Western encounters begin with the imaginative German Jesuit scholar Athanasius Kircher (1602-1680), who produced the first pictorial reconstruction based mainly on Herodotus' account. At the centre Kircher placed a maze, perhaps inspired by Roman labyrinth mosaics, and surrounded it with the twelve courts described by Herodotus. Although various places near the Faiyum Lake were hypothetically linked to the site of the Labyrinth, the identification with Hawara was generally accepted after another Jesuit, Frenchman Claude Sicard, made this proposal at the beginning of the Eighteenth Century.[7]

In 1843 the German explorer Karl Richard Lepsius was apparently the first to narrow down the connection between surviving structures at Hawara and the Labyrinth of the Classical accounts, although he had actually traced the walls of much later structures rather the Middle Kingdom core of Amenemhat's temple itself. Petrie's 1888-90 excavations confirmed the association between the large stone structure in the area south of the pyramid and the vast building of legend. The present name of the site derives from the Labyrinth itself: the ancient name, Hwt-wrt (meaning 'the great mansion', a designation of the temple rather than the pyramid) comes down via Demotic and Greek to the present 'Hawara'. The modern Arabic place name Hawara el-Maqta ('Hawara (of) the quarry') refers to the edifice as a source of stone, providing a tantalising explanation of the almost entirely ruined state of the structure today.

Petrie at Hawara

Petrie would have been familiar with the Classical accounts that spoke of the wondrous Labyrinth, and he was aware of a number of previous excavators at Hawara. These considerations would, at least in part, have motivated his choice of location for his next prospective concession from the Egyptian antiquities authorities. His excavations were set to create much new knowledge about Hawara and contribute to its reputation as a source of spectacular finds. Such was the fame of the site by 1896 that Classicist David G. Hogarth was caused to bemoan:[8]

'It must be for want of comparison also that Egyptology is spoken of so habitually by its votaries as if there were no other archaeology, and that discoveries in Egypt are qualified by absolute superlatives. In the Nilotic mist Mycenae, Nineveh and Pompeii are forgotten, and Hawara or Dahshur extolled as the spots where explorers' eyes have seen the most wonderful resurrections of a bygone age'.

Petrie opens his published account of his first excavations at Hawara in 1888 by noting that Eugène Grébaud, the French head of the Antiquities Service between 1886-1892, had 'decided on allotting the Fayum province to me; it was not being worked by anyone else – the department of antiquities not having touched it for quarter of a century.'

This description belies the fact that Hawara had been an objective of Petrie's for some time. His friend and founder of the Egypt Exploration Fund Amelia Edwards, in a letter of January 19th 1887 to Petrie, describes Manchester industrialist Jesse Haworth as 'just the man who might be got to undertake the excavation of the Labyrinth.' And ultimately it was through Haworth's support that much important Hawara material entered the collections of Manchester Museum at the University of Manchester.

Petrie began work at Hawara in January 1888. Begrudging the lack of British or Egyptian government support, he pointedly noted in his excavation report that 'the present exploration is a private enterprise, assisted by two friends, Mr Jesse Haworth and Mr Martyn Kennard, who independently came forward, and bore the larger portion of the costs.' A certain resentment is obvious on Petrie's part regarding the (relatively recently established) finds division (or 'partage') system. Petrie complains that the Egyptian government takes 'a large proportion of what I find for the Bulak museum, as a toll for the permission to excavate. If only that museum was a safe place…'[9] Petrie was to export a significant proportion of his Hawara finds abroad.

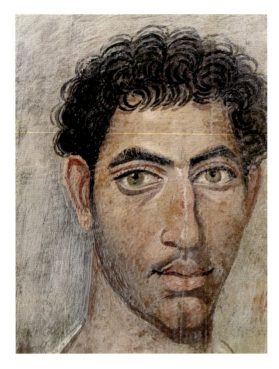

2nd Century AD encaustic-on-wood mummy portrait of a young man, from Hawara (Manchester Museum No. 2263).

2nd Century AD encaustic-on-wood mummy portrait of a mature woman, from Hawara (Manchester Museum No. 2266).

Although undoubtedly attracted by the legendary labyrinth, with a primary mission to 'attack' the interior of Amenemhat's pyramid (in order to definitively identify its royal owner) and excavate some impressive Late Period shaft tombs, Petrie's discovery of the Graeco-Roman necropolis surrounding the pyramid would occupy most of his time and resources. In his own words, 'Though I came for the pyramid, I soon found a mine of interest in the portraits on the mummies.'[10]

The archaeological context of the Graeco-Roman necropolis – mostly located in the area north of the pyramid – was not well recorded by Petrie. What limited detail he did give about his finds has been used to piece together something of the archaeological situation of the mummies.[11] A major obstacle to interpreting the site was that the locations in which the mummies came to be deposited were likely to have reused earlier (largely mudbrick) structures that had themselves been damaged by quarrying activity, so any stratigraphy – even if it had been carefully recorded – would be complicated at best. As it was, Petrie did not in fact employ stratigraphic methods at all in Egypt, only in his work in Palestine.

Skulls bobbing on the waves

Petrie noted the advantages of staying some distance from local villages – with their attendant 'loafers', who were best avoided – and instead set up camp near the excavation site.[12] In a sketch drawn to illustrate a letter home to supporters, Petrie's tent adjoined an area labelled the 'skullery', where human remains – especially interesting skulls linked to portrait mummies – were kept. Elsewhere in his journals, Petrie describes the area as 'a deadhouse for my mummy friends', claiming 'the amount of mummification on my premises is embarrassing'.[13] Later Petrie would recall that 'important mummies were put under my bed' – prompting the disgust of the valet of visiting sponsor Martyn Kennard at living among 'a crowd of mummies'.[14]

Petrie's accounts of the Hawara excavations count among his more intrepid adventures. In particular, the 1888-89 clearance of Late Period tombs gives a glimpse of a sort of proto-Indiana Jones at work. A number of deep tomb shafts at Hawara led to several underground chambers containing intact burials although the organic contents of these had largely been damaged by a high water table.

One sarcophagus was found to be flanked by two concealed compartments, each containing a large number of ushabti figures – substitutes or servants for the deceased. Told by workmen of the discovery of 'images as big as candles', an excited Petrie rushed to the scene. Entering the tomb via a shaft was like the 'descent into Hades', Petrie recounted, and required him to strip off his clothes in order to plunge into the foul water of one of the subterranean burial chambers. Because of its brackish nature, Petrie had to keep his head above the water level and try to dislodge the ushabti figures with his feet, 'while sculls bobbed around on the waves'.[15]

The ushabtis he recovered – 399 in all – were of exceptional quality. They belonged to a man called Horudja, a priest of the goddess Neith – the divine mother of Sobek, the crocodile god of the Faiyum region, who both had an active cult at Hawara. Made of faience and of between 19 and 24 centimetres in height, the ushabtis ranged in colour from olive green to white due to the waterlogged conditions of the tomb. Although Petrie originally believed the ushabtis to date to the Twenty Sixth Dynasty, the style of the figures identify them as the work of the Thirtieth Dynasty (380-343 BC).

Petrie describes the assemblage with an uncharacteristic sense of wonder: 'Next morning, I gazed on the great stack of ushabtis in my tent, as a sort of solidified phantasy; they are about the biggest, the finest, and the greatest pile that I have ever seen of such.'[16]

Ever willing to experiment with conservation techniques, Petrie recorded in his journal entry for the week 13-19th January 1889 that the ushabtis had repeatedly to be soaked in water to remove the salts from them. With typical fastidiousness, Petrie sorted the ushabtis according to workmanship and speculated that seventeen moulds were used. Horudja's 399 ushabtis are now dispersed in collections around the world, with the largest single group – of 58 examples – housed in Manchester Museum.[17]

Perhaps because of their impressive subterranean architecture and interesting contents, these Late Period tombs receive detailed descriptions from Petrie.[18] The archaeologist initially anticipated much more in the way of Middle Kingdom finds, to match the date of the pyramid, noting in his first week on site 'a vast quantity of pit tombs, many unopened, and these may I hope be earlier. There ought to be XII Dyn. tombs here'.[19] During the remainder of his time at Hawara it was, however, Ptolemaic and Roman material that predominated. Petrie's plan of the site shows clusterings in the areas to the north and west of the pyramid enclosure. Plentiful numbers of sacred crocodile mummies, intended as votive gifts to the principal local deity Sobek, were deposited en masse in the Late and Ptolemaic Periods. [20]

Among the human burials, Petrie recognised a development that generally still generally pertains today:[21] Ptolemaic mummies had a greater tendency to be provided with coffins than later Roman ones; most mummies were considered 'plain' – i.e. lacking masks or other cartonnage decorations; and portrait mummies, which were Roman in date, were generally without grave goods. What few items were found associated with graves represent a range of object types, notably glass vessels presumably for unguents.[22] The exact find spots for most of these objects is, regrettably, not recorded.

Compared to finds ascribed an earlier date (a 'pure Egyptian period'), Petrie was unimpressed with the Ptolemaic burials. Bodies were often 'not well mummified' and provided with 'rude' coffins; where the carpentry was good, 'Demotic scrawls' identified the occupant; while bandaging could be 'careful' or even 'beautifully regular', several mummies might be 'successively thrust into one coffin.'[23] The hieroglyphic texts, 'nearly always blundered', on funerary decorations suffered a 'rapid decay' due to the 'falling of the trade into foreign hands' leading to 'mere nonsense' during the Roman Period.

While it is easy to deride Petrie for his opinions – which were, admittedly, common at the time – it is clear that they were significant in establishing a system of values that has endured in Egyptological thinking.

Throughout his descriptions of both Ptolemaic and Roman burials emerges Petrie's distaste for 'gaudy' decorative motifs – particularly the application of gold leaf. In his earliest published discussion of the material, Petrie offers a positive appraisal of a group of three gilded children's mummies: 'Two little girls had the gilt bust with arms beautifully modelled … and stones were inlaid in the jewellery.' In a letter of early March 1888 describing the same event, Petrie is somewhat more judgemental: 'An awful day of mummies. First thing, while going my rounds before breakfast, I found Muhd in a hole hauling out gilt-faced things. There were two little girls, quite too splendaciously got up. All head, bust and arms of moulded stucco, gilt all over' but he acknowledged 'the girls are really superior beings, as good a work as one could have in such a style.'[24]

Later the same month, as many more examples appeared, Petrie complained that 'the plague of gilt mummies continues', 'wretched things with gilt faces and painted head pieces' – singling out a cartonnage cover with Greek inscription as 'interesting, not only for the name but as showing that all these gaudy and ignorantly painted cartonnages were probably made by Greeks and not by Egyptians.'[25]

When, in March 1888, he was first overwhelmed with 'gilt-faced things', Petrie tellingly remarks: 'I suppose I must bring them all away, as they will be worth something in England, in spite of their hideously late style. I am not sure but what their gilt gaudiness may be very attractive to British Philistines.'[26] Here is an explicit acknowledgement that, despite his own disdain, Petrie saw a commercial opportunity for his finds in the West. Indeed, he wrote to a sponsor, Rev. Aquila Dodgson on 4th December 1888 from his second season at Hawara, regarding a collector named Mr Leigh in England: 'If I cannot get a ritual [i.e. a mummy] at Boulak he [Mr Leigh] might perhaps be content with one of the gilt-faced creatures of Ptolemaic era.'[27] Mention of the Egyptian Museum at Boulak may be a reference to the Sale Room of the Museum which operated in some form from 1883 until 1979.[28] There was clearly a system of relative value dependent on appearance; echoing Herodotus' reports of the costs of performing mummification, Petrie wrote to a sponsor in 1891 that it cost '£5 for a plain mummy; £10 for a fancy one.'[29]

Even during the Autumn of 1888, his second season at Hawara, Petrie describes the discovery there by 'Faraq, the Arab dealer' of 'a lot of the common gilt masks, such as I did not care to go on looking for.'[30]By 1911, Petrie was obliged, he claimed, to leave on site 'many gilt bust mummies' because they were 'mostly too rotted to move'. [31]

While gilded funerary trappings proved to be somewhat of a bugbear for Petrie because of their ubiquity, he certainly knew of the enthusiasm for – and valuable expertise regarding – textiles amongst his friends in the north of England. He wrote to Rev. Aquila Dodgson from Hawara in April 1888: 'Pray inform your good friend Mr Bradbury that he shall have the examination of all the patterned cloths if he likes… I shall much value a technical report on them'.[32]

The finest set of Hawara textiles were 'all soaked cleaned and ironed', packed up and sent to Manchester,[33]with a representative selection sent to other British industrial centres like Bolton and Sheffield. Petrie does not specify the source of most of the 'textiles', but they must almost exclusively have derived from mummy wrappings.

The value of these specimens for display to a public very familiar with the textile industry was not lost on the mill-owning sponsors of Petrie's excavations, and samples were in turn used to generate further enthusiasm for archaeological work. In 1912, the cotton magnate Jesse Haworth displayed a range of linen textiles from Petrie's 1887-9 excavations at Hawara at a meeting of the Manchester Egyptian and Oriental Society, making explicit the link with the modern British textile industry and likening these 'remarkable cloths' to those 'which are now produced weekly in their thousands in Lancashire'.[34]Egyptian cotton directly supplied the mills of the north-west of England, and provided a distinctive lens with which to view the achievements of the ancient past for an audience well familiar with warps and wefts.

Retrieving and interpreting

Work at Hawara, as at other sites in Egypt, was undertaken by hundreds of Egyptian men, women and children who are hardly ever named in publications.[35]British excavations were also enabled by the colonial infrastructure of the country. Petrie renders thanks in his excavation report to English official Major Hewat, the inspector of public works in the Faiyum province, for 'the mummies and antiquities having been stowed week by week in his office as I gradually dispatched them'[36]– an important hint at the logistical support that was possible in a country under a British mandate. Throughout his writing, Petrie contrasts Western order and expertise, facilitated by colonial apparatus, with his workmen's emotion, anxiousness, and general untrustworthiness;[37]thus tip money ('bakhshish') is the incentive that 'stimulates discovery'.[38]Contradictions are inherent here. Deriding one transactional relationship, he espouses another.

First Century AD gilded-plaster & painted-cartonnage mummy of a lady named Isaious, from Hawara (Manchester Museum No. 11630).

Hawara painted-cartonnage fragment of a Ptolemaic man
named Nimaatre (Manchester Museum No. 2112).

Despite Petrie's projection of a meticulous, methodical approach, he himself cherry-picked from the site and prized mummies that gave a return: 'I opened some dozens of shafts but only one repaid the work'.[39] Graeco-Roman mummies with any form of decoration made up only around two per cent of those excavated;[40] the majority being undecorated - 'plain' – specimens, and Petrie was ruthlessly efficient in working through these, claiming: 'as for poor mummies without painting or cases, we heave them over by the dozen every day.'[41]

For those mummies that Petrie did deem worthy of saving he experimented with conservation techniques, notably the application of 'spoonfuls' of paraffin wax to consolidate fragile surfaces and to 'remedy the dullness' of some of the portraits.[42] Some mummies are seen in a photograph of 1911 with their portraits shielded from the hot sun with newspaper, and some were said to be laid out on the deck of a ship on the way back to England to dry in the sun.[43] Petrie justified the removal of portraits from some mummies as a way of preserving them from damage during transport[44] and indeed replaced several in cases of well-preserved mummies when both reached museums.[45]

Petrie's fieldwork became widely known in the UK and elsewhere, due in no small measure to his prolific attempts to increase his profile in order to raise funds. Petrie chose the location and timing of his annual exhibition of finds particularly carefully; in June-July 1888, in a departure from his usual venue at Oxford Mansions in London, the Hawara finds were on display in the theatrical surroundings of the Egyptian Hall in the same city's Piccadilly district, with Petrie providing tantalising previews to the quality press – with visitors including the orientalist painter Lawrence Alma-Tadema and perhaps even Oscar Wilde, whose novella The Picture of Dorian Gray may have drawn inspiration from the hauntingly handsome young men in the Faiyum portraits.[46] Of the exhibition, Petrie reported to Amelia Edwards:

'Things have gone very well at the hall, in spite of the miserable weather…I expect that we shall take about £100 (2000) people… So that is better than I had hoped for… several solid folks have been … all more than once. We have got hold of the right vein of folks, + not had any nasty boors or 'arrys about'.[47]

Such exhibitions of finds, and the press coverage they received, cemented Petrie's reputation as 'hero archaeologist', bringing 'home' a rich trawl of finds. His energetic endeavours – camping on-site, delving into dangerous subterranean tombs, and unearthing spectacular treasures – are nowhere clearer than in accounts of his time at Hawara. These would undoubtedly go on to inform popular perceptions of archaeological work into the Twentieth Century. However, it is clear that Petrie himself did not act alone, as his reports often suggest, nor did he do most of the 'discovering'; the large Egyptian workforce he employed only features incidentally in his own narratives, and then usually to be admonished for some shortcoming or emotion. He himself displayed obvious bias about his finds – and his impressions have reverberated in Egyptological assessments of Graeco-Roman material ever since. Petrie used connections with specific British officials, and colonial apparatus in general – not least the partage system – to transport objects to an eager public in the West. It is perhaps little wonder, then, that in the first three of Sax Rohmer's wildly orientalising Fu Manchu books (1913-17), a key British bulwark against the evil Oriental title character is named 'Dr. Petrie.'[48]

Roman-period glass vessel from Hawara (Manchester Museum No. 2068).

| NOTES |

This is an abridged version of one chapter of a book entitled 'Golden Mummies, Painted Faces' to accompany a major international touring exhibition of Graeco-Roman funerary material from Manchester Museum. 'Golden Mummies of Egypt' opens at the Buffalo Museum of Science on 8th February 2020.

1. M. Lehner, 1997. The Complete Pyramids. London: Thames and Hudson, 181-183.

2. For a possible reconstruction of the complex, see E. P. Uphill, 2000. Pharaoh's Gateway to Eternity: the Hawara labyrinth of King Amenemhat III. Studies in Egyptology. London; New York: Kegan Paul International.

3. On the cult of Amenemhat III at Hawara during the Graeco-Roman Period, and for a comprehensive survey of the site in general, see I. Uytterhoeven 2009. Hawara in the Graeco-Roman period: life and death in a Fayum village. Orientalia Lovaniensia Analecta 174. Leuven: Peeters, 423-448.

4. Histories, Book II, 148; see D. Asheri, A. B. Lloyd, and A., Corcella. 2007. A Commentary on Herodotus Books I-IV. Cambridge: Cambridge University Press, 348-350 for commentary, with conjectural reconstruction of structure described in Herodotus, Pliny and Strabo.

5. The classic study is A. B. Lloyd, 1970. The Egyptian Labyrinth. *Journal of Egyptian Archaeology* 56, 81-100. See also Uytterhoeven 2009, 238-247.

6. See C. Malleson. 2019. *The Fayum Landscape. Ten Thousand Years of Archaeology, Texts and Traditions in Egypt*. Cairo: American University in Cairo Press, 147-187, within the wider context of perceptions of the Faiyum.

7. Uytterhoeven 2009, 1.

8. D. G. Hogarth, 1896. *A Wandering Scholar in the Levant*. London, John Murray, 171-2.

9. W. M. Flinders Petrie. 1889. *Hawara, Biahmu and Arsinoe*. London: Field & Tuer, 3-4.

10. Many events such as this recorded in exhibition reports are retold with more flourish in Petrie's autobiography: W. M. Flinders Petrie, 1931. *Seventy Years in Archaeology*. London: Low, Marston & Co., 83.

11. Uytterhoeven 2009, 183-237; P. C. Roberts. 2007. An archaeological context for British discoveries of mummy portraits in the Fayum. In J. Picton, S. Quirke, and P. C. Roberts (eds), *Living Images: Egyptian funerary portraits in the Petrie Museum*, 13-57. Walnut Creek, CA: Left Coast Press.

12. Petrie 1889, 3.

13. Roberts 2007, 23.

14. A lively discussion of this episode occurs in Petrie 1931, 82.

15. W. M. Flinders Petrie. 1890. *Kahun, Gurob and Hawara*. London: Kegan Paul, Trench, Trübner, and Co., 9.

16. Petrie 1890, 9.

17. On the shabtis of Horudja, see G. Janes, 2012. *The Shabti Collections 5: A Selection from the Manchester Museum*. Cheshire: Olicar House, 392-434. For Horudja's family tree based on finds from Hawara, see Uytterhoeven 2009, 511-512.

18. For example, Petrie 1890, 8-11.

19. Journal 22-29 January 1888: Roberts 2007, 84.

20. Mentioned also by Herodotus (II, 148), the deposits of crocodile mummies underlay the Graeco-Roman human graves Petrie excavated: Petrie 1889, 17.

21. Petrie 1889, 14-21.

22. Similar small glass vessels were found in association with contemporary mummies at Bahariya Oasis: Z. Hawass, 2000. *The Valley of the Golden Mummies*. New York: Harry Abrams, 73.

23. For Petrie's account, see Petrie 1889, 14-17.

24. Petrie's journal of 4 March 1888: Roberts 2007, 94. Petrie recounts the same wording in his autobiography: Petrie 1931, 88.

25. Petrie's journal of March 1888: Roberts 2007, 39.

26. Petrie's journal of 18-24 March 1888: Roberts 2007, 96.

27. B. Moon. 2005. ' "A Fearful Outbreak of Egyptology" in the North West', Paper read at the ASTENE conference, Manchester. Unpublished., 6.

28. On the rather over-looked operations of the Cairo Museum Sale Room, see P. Piacentini, 2013-2014. 'The antiquities path: from the Sale Room of the Egyptian Museum in Cairo, through dealers, to private and public collections. A work in progress.' *Egyptian & Egyptological Documents, Archives, Libraries* 4, 105-130.

29. H. Forrest 2011. *Manufacturers, mummies and Manchester: two hundred years of interest in and study of Egyptology in the greater Manchester area.* BAR British Series 532. Oxford: Archaeopress, 27.

30. Petrie's journal of October 1888: Roberts 2007, 23.

31. Petrie's journal from 26 February 1911: Roberts and Quirke 2007, 104.

32. Moon 2005, 3

33. Petrie 1889, 4: 'the most important and complete set technologically going to a Manchester museum.'

34. W.M. Crompton, 1913. 'Report of the Manchester Egyptian and Oriental Society, 1913.' *Journal of the Manchester Egyptian and Oriental Society* 2, 12.

35. On these 'hidden hands', see S. Quirke. 2010. Hidden hands: Egyptian workforces in Petrie excavation archives 1880-1924. Duckworth Egyptology. London: Duckworth

36. Petrie 1889, 4.

37. For example, 'no native would treat the place with sufficient tenderness to avoid loosening the bricks overhead' (Petrie 1890, 6); thefts at Hawara were said to be common (Petrie 1931, 90).

38. Petrie 1889, 3.

39. Petrie 1889, 8.

40. Uytterhoeven 2009, 22 and n. 58.

41. Petrie's journal, 29 January – 5 February 1888: P.C. Roberts, and S. Quirke. 2007. Extracts from the Petrie Journals. In J. Picton, Janet, S. Quirke, and P. C. Roberts (eds), *Living Images: Egyptian funerary portraits in the Petrie Museum*, 83-104. Walnut Creek, CA: Left Coast Press84.

42. Petrie 1889, 19

43. Petrie 1931, 89.

44. Roberts 2007, 29.

45. Roberts 2007, 87.

46. D. Montserrat, 1998. Unidentified human remains: mummies and the erotics of biography. In D. Montserrat (ed.), *Changing bodies, changing meanings: studies on the human body in antiquity*, London; New York: Routledge, 162-197.

47. Petrie to Edwards, 12 July 1888.

48. See R. Luckhurst, 2012. *The Mummy's Curse: the true history of a dark fantasy*. Oxford: Oxford University Press, 168-9.

对皮特里在哈瓦拉的工作的重新评估

1888 ～ 1911 年间，威廉·马修·弗林德斯·皮特里（1853 ～ 1942 年）带领考古队在法尤姆地区南端的哈瓦拉遗址开展了为期三年的考古发掘工作。坎贝尔·普赖斯在本文中提到，重新审视从这些考古活动中发掘、挑选和倒运的文物及其相关档案，可以对皮特里所秉持的目标和采用的方法提供一个新的研究视角。

皮特里并未在其公开发表的报道中明确提及自己此前为何会对哈瓦拉遗址感兴趣。1887 年春，积极进取的作家阿米莉亚·爱德华兹在某次与皮特里交流的过程中，提起了一位富有的潜在资助人，杰西·霍沃斯（一位曼彻斯特的棉花实业家），说他"是那种可能愿意发掘'迷宫'的人"。"迷宫"是埃及古典文献中记载的一种类似于传说的建筑，它的灵感源自曾经统治过该地区的一个中王国时代金字塔神庙群的遗迹。皮特里与爱德华兹之间的通信揭示了一张由英国的帝国关系、顾虑与便利所结成的错综复杂的关系网——对这则故事进行剖析并尝试向埃及和英国的观众进行解释已经变得越来越重要。

皮特里似乎是在英国科学促进会于曼彻斯特举办的一次聚会上第一次见到霍沃斯的。促进会与伦敦大学学院著名的优生学家弗朗西斯·高尔顿共同资助了一场研究旅行。通过这场旅行，皮特里为 1887 年出版的《埃及古迹的种族摄影集》一书收集了资料。此后，霍沃斯成为皮特里主要的私人资助者之一，曼彻斯特博物馆也因此获得了许多重要的古埃及文物藏品。

1888 年初抵达哈瓦拉后，皮特里立即"发掘"了上述金字塔神庙群，并确认其主人是阿蒙涅姆赫特三世（约公元前 1831- 前 1786 年）。皮特里对没能找到更多的中王国遗迹感到失望——甚至就连"迷宫"的主要结构都未曾发现。不过，他在考古方面的注意力完全被后王国时期以及"希腊 - 罗马"时期的陪葬品所占据，特别是那些以金箔和 / 或彩绘画像装饰的木乃伊。

大规模的发掘工作离不开大批埃及工人，然而公开出版的书面叙述只将他们一笔带过。皮特里在自己的笔记中记录了一些工人的名字——例如，名叫哈利法和阿里·哈马德的工人在 1910-1911 年的发掘工作中做出了重大发现——但除此之外，当地的埃及人似乎成为了安全、冷静的考古实践的障碍。皮特里发现了与当地村庄保持一定

皮特里写给阿米莉亚 · 爱德华兹的信，1888 年 4 月 9 日。现藏于 EES 档案馆

距离的好处，以及最好避开那些闻风而来的"游手好闲的人"。他在1888年4月9日写给阿米莉亚·爱德华兹的信中画了一张草图，描绘了自己的帐篷"营地",旁边有一块标记"头骨室"字样的区域，那里存放着人类遗骸——尤其是从有彩绘画像的木乃伊上取下来的有趣的头骨。皮特里曾在其他场合把这个地方称作"我那些木乃伊朋友的停尸间"，并表示"我这里的木乃伊数量令人尴尬"。

尽管皮特里极力驳斥关于他从资助人那里得到的"只是用于购买文物的钱"这种说法，但他显然对自己送给资助人的文物的潜在价值有所关注。他对"黄金木乃伊'狂热'"和"带着黄金面具和彩绘头饰的可怜东西"颇有微词。然而，到了1888年3月，虽然很无奈，皮特里开始抢救这些木乃伊："我想我必须把它们都带走，虽说它们都是可憎的晚期风格，但在英国肯定值钱。我感觉这种镀金的俗丽风格可能对英国那些市侩非常有吸引力。"皮特里显然已经意识到，一些英国资助人对《圣经》与埃及考古学之间的联系有着浓厚的兴趣。例如，杰西·霍沃斯就是曼彻斯特基督教新教徒团体的重要成员，该团体在维多利亚晚期的英国拥有相当大的政治影响力。

从统计数字来看，在罗马时期的木乃伊上发现彩绘画像的概率并不高——皮特里声称，只有大约2%的木乃伊有这种画像——但这些栩栩如生的"肖像"却对西方的审美情趣产生了重大影响。由于此前"挖出了"数百具未经装饰的木乃伊，他认为"从人类学的角度来看，这些发现十分重要，它们通过画像将这些人的肤色和特征生动地保存了下来。"这类种族脸谱化的尝试，是假定这些画像就是面具之下的木乃伊生前的模拟画像，而这是一个尚待确认的"事实"，包括本文作者在内的众多反对者认为，应将这种"肖像"解释为标准化且理想化的画像，而且最有可能是在逝者死后绘制的。然而，皮特里对这些画像"真实性"的评价与其对整个哈瓦拉地区墓葬艺术质量的普遍贬损相辅相成。对皮特里来说，"这些华而不实的彩绘木乃伊棺可能不是由埃及人制作的，而是希腊人。"他因未能找到"纯粹"的埃及艺术而感到遗憾。

1911年，在结束最后一次考古发掘后，皮特里撰写了优生论著作《文明的革命》。他在其中进一步哀叹道，"希腊和罗马艺术与埃及艺术格格不入，完全不足以支撑埃及的艺术设计。再也找不到那种古老的风格了。"鉴于这本书的主题是避免"种族融合"，皮特里对"希腊-罗马"时期墓葬的看法带着一种特殊的殖民焦虑。他在《文明的革命》一书中总结道，"然而，如果人们很容易就能理解，每种文明的源头都存在于种族的融合之中，那么，也许优生学能在未来的一些文明中精心分离出优良的种族，禁止其继续融合，直到他们形成一个独特的种族类型，并在移居他处之后开启新的文明。人类未来的进步可能既有赖于为创建一个种族而实施的隔离，也取决于创建之后的种族融合。"

皮特里对古埃及"希腊-罗马"时期艺术的矛盾态度让我们有机会深入了解他更广泛的思想：一方面，他相信融合与冲突可以带来进步;另一方面，他又不喜不同风格混合之后所产生的明显不协调的"华而不实"之感。这里的大背景是英国对埃及的殖民控制，它促成并推动了皮特里的考古研究——尽管面对忘恩负义的埃及与英国政府的管理时，他始终坚持科学是公正的。

"帝国的焦虑"已经被证实是几部哥特式恐怖小说的灵感源泉。因此在萨克斯·罗默

来自哈瓦拉的儿童黄金木乃伊，公元1-2世纪。（曼彻斯特博物馆，藏品编号2109）

具有狂热东方化色彩的"傅满洲系列"小说中，英国对抗东方威胁的中坚人物被命名为"皮特里博士"也许就不足为奇了。弗林德斯·皮特里在哈瓦拉与其他地方的工作，直接或间接地受益于英国对埃及的控制。尽管并未明确承认，但英国（以及其他欧洲国家）还是效仿了古罗马对埃及的统治。在奥古斯都时期的硬币上，埃及被喻为一只强大但却丧失抵抗力的鳄鱼，并伴随着拉丁文 AEGYPTO CAPTA（"被占领的埃及"）的字样，而庞奇在 1882 年创作的漫画也采用了同样的"他者"意象。

这种政治控制形式也许可以解释皮特里对埃及工人在哈瓦拉发现的"希腊 - 罗马"时期墓葬的矛盾心理。这凸显了随葬品的出土、选择和解读并不是孤立的，也不是在知识真空的环境中发生的。皮特里对希腊、罗马和埃及这三种观念能够以令人惊讶的方式共存感到矛盾；他选择将不同类型的墓葬与某些民族联系在一起。事实上，无论是种族还是"人种"都不像皮特里所设想的那样，是与生俱来的生物特征，而是社会构建，以及竞争的产物。

"希腊 - 罗马"时期那些有着面覆黄金面具和彩绘画像的木乃伊的草鞋上绘有"五花大绑"的逝者仇敌的形象，情况的复杂性可以从中窥见一斑。这些绘在木乃伊身上的人可以通过不同且不可知的方式被认定为埃及人、希腊人或罗马人。尽管借用了源于法老的标准排外意象，但"被缚的俘虏"是一个神奇并且具有辟邪功效的胜利主题，极其适用于墓葬中——这不是对某一个体的偏见，也不是原本以为过去存在不平等现象的证据。

虽然嘲讽皮特里关于"希腊 - 罗马"时期木乃伊装饰"华而不实"的评论不是什么难事，但他对哈瓦拉考古发现的最初解读对埃及学和其他领域都产生了深远的影响。这种主观论断应该强调以古埃及"艺术"评估为基础的更广泛的假设；表面上看来，法老时代的艺术风格和自我呈现依然受人青睐与接受，使得（后代或当代）其他未能完全符合这一标准的东西都显得陌生且具有"他者"的色彩，从而加剧和延续了古老的偏见。在最极端的情况下，人们常引用这种高度程式化的古代战斗场景来为明显的种族主义态度辩护。

重新审视皮特里的研究不是通过简单地批判一个人的观点来试图点亮我们自己的道德良知；而应成为促使我们积极反思自己的知识构建和传播体系的缘由，以及通过物品来讲述更复杂故事的挑战。

来自哈瓦拉的一位名叫伊索斯的女士的木乃伊有装饰图案的足盒，公元 2 世纪。（曼彻斯特博物馆，藏品编号 11630）

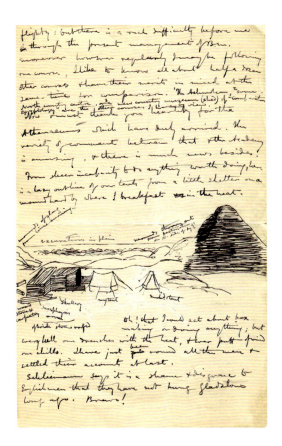

Letter from W. M. F. Petrie to Amelia Edwards, 9 April 1888, today in the EES Archives.

William Matthew Flinders Petrie (1853–1942) directed three seasons of excavations at the site of Hawara, on the southern edge of the Faiyum region, between 1888 and 1911. A re-examination of the objects excavated, selected and distributed from these campaigns, and their associated archival imprint, offers a new perspective on the aims and methods employed, writes Campbell Price.

Petrie's own prior interest in the site of Hawara is somewhat obscured in his own published accounts. In an exchange in spring 1887 between Petrie and Amelia Edwards, the enterprising author describes a wealthy potential sponsor, Jesse Haworth (a Manchester cotton industrialist), as 'just the man that might be got to excavate the Labyrinth', a quasilegendary structure described in Classical accounts of Egypt and inspired by remains of a Middle Kingdom pyramid temple complex that once dominated the site. The correspondence between Petrie and Edwards betrays a complex cotton-spun web of British Imperial connections, concerns and convenience – a story that it is increasingly important to unpick and attempt to explain to audiences in Egypt and the UK.

Petrie appears to have first met Haworth in Manchester at a gathering of the British Association for the Advancement of Science, an organisation that – along with additional support from prominent UCL eugenicist Francis Galton – funded a research trip to allow Petrie to collect data for his 1887 volume Racial Photographs from the Egyptian Monuments. Haworth went on to be one of Petrie's main private backers, resulting in many significant Egyptology acquisitions for Manchester Museum.

Once at Hawara in early 1888, and after 'attacking' the pyramid to confirm the identity of the owner as Amenemhat III (c. 1831–1786 BCE), Petrie was disappointed by the lack of further Middle Kingdom remains – with even the main structure of the 'Labyrinth' remaining elusive. Instead, his archaeological attention was monopolised by funerary material of the Late and Graeco-Roman Periods, notably in the form of mummies richly decorated with gold-leaf and/or painted wooden panel 'portraits'.

The presence of Egyptian workers that enabled such labour on so large a scale is fleeting in printed accounts. Petrie does record the names of some individual workers in his notebooks – for example men named Khalifa and Ali Hamad as making significant finds in the 1910-11 season – but otherwise local Egyptians appear as an impediment to the practice of safe and dispassionate archaeology. Petrie noted the advantages of staying at some distance from local villages, with their attendant 'loafers' who were best to be avoided. A sketch in one of his letters to Amelia Edwards, dated 9 April 1888 and now in the EES archives, illustrates Petrie's tented 'camp' with an adjoining area labelled the 'skullery', where human remains – especially interesting skulls derived from portrait mummies – were kept. Elsewhere Petrie described the area as 'a deadhouse for my mummy friends', claiming 'the amount of mummification on my premises is embarrassing.'

Although Petrie fought against the implication that subscriptions to his work from donors were 'mere purchase money', he clearly had an eye on the potential value of finds to his supporters. He complained of 'a plague of gilt mummies', 'wretched things with gilt faces and painted head pieces.' By March 1888, however, Petrie was resigned to salvaging them: 'I suppose I must bring them all away, as they will be worth something in England, in spite of their hideously late style. I am not sure but what their gilt gaudiness may be very attractive to British Philistines.' Petrie was clearly aware of the considerable interest that existed amongst some British subscribers in Biblical connections wi th Egyptian archaeology. Jesse Haworth was, for example, a prominent member of the Non-conformist Protestant community in Manchester, a group that held considerable political influence in late Victorian Britain.

The discovery of the painted panels on Roman Period mummies was statistically uncommon – Petrie claimed only around 2 percent of mummies had such decoration – but these strikingly lifelike 'portraits' had a major impact on Western aesthetic tastes. While he 'heaved over' hundreds of undecorated mummies, Petrie reasoned it to be 'a great point anthropologically to have skulls of persons whose living appearance as to colour and feature is preserved to us by the portraits.' Such attempts at racial profiling assumed the paintings to be mimetic representations of the mummified people they masked; this is a farfrom- established 'fact', with numerous dissenters including the present writer favouring the interpretation

Gilded mummy of a small child from Hawara, 1st-2nd century CE (Manchester Museum No. 2109)

of such 'portraits' as standardised, idealised and most likely posthumous. Yet Petrie's appraisals of the 'truth' of the paintings went hand-in-hand with a generally pejorative view of the artistic quality of material from Hawara as a whole. For Petrie, 'all these gaudy and ignorantly painted cartonnages were probably made by Greeks and not by Egyptians'. He regretted the lack of 'pure' Egyptian art.

In his 1911 eugenicist tract *Revolutions of Civilization*, written at the close of his third and final Hawara season, Petrie further laments: 'Greek and Roman art was too incongruous to be a prop to Egyptian design, and the old style passed away forever'. Given the entire book is about the avoidance of 'racial mixing', Petrie's opinions about Graeco-Roman funerary material take on a particular sense of colonial anxiety. In *Revolutions*, Petrie concludes: 'Yet if the view becomes readily grasped, that the source of every civilisation has lain in race mixture, it may be that eugenics will, in some future civilisation, carefully segregate fine races, and prohibit continual mixture, until they have a distinct type, which will start a new civilisation when transplanted. The future progress of man may depend as much on isolation to establish a type, as of fusion of types when established.'

Petrie's ambivalence towards Graeco-Roman art gives an insight into his broader thinking: on one hand, he believed admixture and strife brought about progress, yet was appalled by the 'gaudiness' of the apparent disjunction produced by the mixing of different styles. The wider context here is British colonial control of Egypt, an infrastructure that allowed and actively enabled Petrie's work – despite his (often still accepted) claims to scientific impartiality in the face of ungrateful Egyptian and British government administration.

Imperial anxieties have already been shown to be at the root of several fictional Gothic horror narratives; it is perhaps unsurprising that in Sax Rohmer's wildly orientalising Fu Manchu-books a key British bulwark against the Oriental threat represented by the title character is named 'Dr. Petrie.' Flinders Petrie's work at Hawara, as elsewhere, benefitted both directly and indirectly from British imperial control of Egypt. Although not explicitly acknowledged, Britain (and other European powers) emulated ancient Roman power over Egypt. The country was personified as a powerful but defenceless crocodile with the Latin words AEGYPTO CAPTA ('Egypt Captured') on coinage of Augustus, while in Punch cartoons of 1882, the same 'other'-ing imagery was deployed.

This form of political control perhaps explains some of Petrie's ambivalence to the Graeco-Roman funerary material that his workers uncovered at Hawara. It makes the point with particular emphasis that the unearthing, selection and interpretation of material does not happen in isolation, nor in an intellectual vacuum. Petrie was conflicted in seeing Greek, Roman and Egyptian concepts coexisting in surprising ways; he chose to identify different types of material with certain ethnicities. In reality, neither ethnicity nor 'race' are innate biological features as Petrie supposed, but are socially constructed – and contested.

The complexity of the situation is illustrated by scenes of enemies of the deceased shown bound under the sandals of both gilded-mask and painted 'portrait mummies' of the Graeco-Roman Period. The individuals on whose mummies these scenes appear could have identified as Egyptian, Greek or Roman in differing and unknowable ways. Although borrowed from standard xenophobic imagery of the pharaoh, the motif of the bound captive is a magical and apotropaic motif of triumph appropriate to funerary sphere – not a statement of the personal prejudices of an individual, nor evidence of assumed inequality in the past.

While it is easy to lampoon Petrie's comments about the 'gaudiness' of Graeco-Roman Period mummy decorations, his initial interpretation of the Hawara finds has cast a long shadow in Egyptology and elsewhere. Such subjective pronouncements should highlight broader assumptions based on assessments of ancient Egyptian 'art'; pharaonic self-presentations continue to be favoured and accepted at face value, making anything else (later or contemporary) that doesn't quite fit seem foreign and 'other', thus compounding and perpetuating ancient biases. In the most extreme cases, highly stylised ancient battle scenes are cited as justification for explicitly racist attitudes.

Re-examining the work of Petrie is not simply a matter of critiquing one man's opinions in an attempt to lighten our own moral conscience; it should be cause to actively reflect on our own systems of knowledge construction and transmission, and a challenge to use objects to tell more complicated stories.

Decorated footcase of the mummy of a lady named Isaious from Hawara, 2nd century CE (Manchester Museum No. 11630)

THE FACE OF ETERNAL LIFE
Egypt and Its Golden Mummies

永恒的面孔
古埃及的黄金木乃伊

多元文化生活
Life in a Multicultural Society

埃及一直与周边的文明保持联系，而不是像人们经常描绘的那样孤立隔绝。在法老的统治下，埃及与埃及南部的努比亚和地中海周围地区的贸易关系已经持续了千百年，许多非埃及人来到埃及生活。但是，这些民族之间的关系并不总是和平的，有时还会有争夺权力的暴力斗争。在"希腊-罗马"时期，其中一些暴力事件被记录在莎草纸文件中。

公元前 305 ～公元前 30 年，源于马其顿的托勒密王朝开始统治埃及。这个王朝的法老把都城建在亚历山大港海岸上，面朝故国，但他们在埃及各地神庙墙上的形象却与传统法老无异。他们在肥沃的法尤姆地区开垦农田，以安置来自希腊的新移民。在这里和其他地方，托勒密王朝提倡崇拜一种新的、多元文化的神——塞拉皮斯（古埃及的一位神）。人们在家里敬奉各种希腊、罗马和埃及的神。通过那些逝者的陪葬品，我们可以更为深入地了解古埃及人民的日常生活。

Egypt was always in contact with neighbouring cultures and was never as isolated as it is often portrayed. Plentiful evidence survives for trade with Nubia to the south of Egypt and around the Mediterranean for centuries under the Pharaohs, and many non-Egyptians came to live in Egypt. But relations between these peoples were not always peaceful and there were sometimes violent struggles for power. During the Graeco-Roman Period, some of these events are recorded in papyrus documents.

A dynasty of Macedonian origin called the Ptolemies ruled Egypt from 305–30 BC. They built their capital on the coast at Alexandria facing their homeland, but they appeared as traditional Pharaohs on temple walls throughout Egypt. They developed farmland in the fertile Faiyum area to house new settlers from Greece. Here and elsewhere the Ptolemies promoted the worship of a new, multi-cultural god called Serapis. A wide range of Greek, Roman and Egyptian gods were worshipped in people's homes. By looking at items found buried with the dead, we can learn more about the everyday lives of the Egyptian people.

埃及、希腊和罗马
Egypt, Greece and Rome

  埃及人已经习惯了外来的统治者。亚历山大大帝只是在埃及以外出生的众多法老中的一位。他在公元前332年来到了埃及，并开启了马其顿-希腊国王对埃及大约三个世纪的统治。公元前30年，随着王朝的最后一位统治者克里奥帕特拉七世去世，埃及在随后的四个世纪里又成为了罗马帝国的一部分。埃及历史上的这一时期通常被称为"希腊-罗马"时期。

Egypt has been accustomed to foreign rulers. Alexander the Great was just one in a line of Pharaohs born outside Egypt. His arrival in 332 BC brought about three centuries of rule by Macedonian-Greek kings called the Ptolemies. With the death of the last ruler of the dynasty – Queen Cleopatra VII – in 30 BC, Egypt became part of the Roman Empire for a further four centuries. This era of Egyptian history is often called the Graeco-Roman Period.

时间表
Timeline

约公元前 6000 年	美索不达米亚和埃及首次利用水利灌溉工程和治理洪水
约公元前 2589 年 - 公元前 2503 年	在吉萨修建了胡夫、哈夫拉和孟卡拉三座金字塔
约公元前 1831 年 - 公元前 1786 年	法老阿蒙涅姆赫特三世统治埃及 45 年, 在哈瓦拉建造了一个庞大的金字塔群
公元前 1184 年	特洛伊陷落
约公元前 450 年	希腊历史学家希罗多德造访了埃及并将哈瓦拉的阿蒙涅姆赫特三世神庙的遗迹形容为是"迷宫"
公元前 332 年	马其顿战士亚历山大大帝来到埃及并成为法老他开创了延续约 300 年的托勒密王朝, 继承了希腊化埃及的统治
公元前 221 年	秦始皇统一中国, 建立秦帝国, 称始皇帝
公元前 30 年	托勒密王朝末代法老克里奥帕特拉七世去世, 埃及成为罗马共和国的一部分
公元 79 年	维苏威火山爆发, 庞贝和赫库兰尼姆城被毁
公元 117 年	罗马皇帝哈德良访问埃及。因画中人的发型, 很多彩绘画像被推测完成于这个时代
公元 476 年 - 公元 480 年	西罗马帝国覆灭
公元 553 年	信奉基督教的拜占庭皇帝查士丁尼一世关闭了菲莱岛的伊希斯神庙, 标志埃及多神教时代的正式结束
公元 646 年	阿拉伯人攻陷埃及, 伊斯兰教成为埃及的主要宗教
约公元 700 年	世界上最大的纪念碑墨西哥乔鲁拉大金字塔竣工
1798 年	法国统帅拿破仑入侵埃及, 敕令编修《埃及志》
1801 年	英国军队打败法国, 并支持奥斯曼帝国对埃及的统治
1882 年	英国海军炮轰亚历山大城, 以确保对苏伊士运河的控制
1888 年	考古学家和埃及古物学家威廉 · 马修 · 弗林德斯 · 皮特里开始在哈瓦拉的考古发掘
1922 年	英国考古学家和埃及古物学家霍华德 · 卡特发现法老图坦卡蒙的陵墓
1956 年	英国对苏伊士运河的直接控制终结

c. 6000 BC	First irrigation and flood control in Mesopotamia and Egypt
c. 2589–2503 BC	Three pyramids of Khufu, Khafre and Menkaure built at Giza
c. 1831–1786 BC	King Amenemhat III rules for 45 years, building a huge pyramid complex at Hawara
1184 BC	Fall of Troy
c. 450 BC	Greek historian Herodotus visits Egypt and describes remains of Amenemhat's temple at Hawara as the 'Labyrinth'
332 BC	Macedonian king warrior Alexander the Great arrives in Egypt and is proclaimed Pharaoh. He is succeeded by a 300-year dynasty of kings called the Ptolemies and inherited the rules of Hellenistic Egypt.
221 BC	Yingzheng, first emperor of China has unified China and created the Great Qin Empire.
30 BC	Death of Queen Cleopatra VII, the last of the Ptolemies. Egypt becomes part of the Roman Republic
AD 79	Eruption of the volcano Vesuvius, and destruction of the cities of Pompeii and Herculaneum
AD 117	The Emperor Hadrian visits Egypt. Many mummy portraits are dated to this period based on the style of their hair
AD 476–480	Fall of the Western Roman Empire
AD 553	Christian Emperor Justinian I closes the Temple of Isis at Philae, signalling the official end of paganism in Egypt
AD 646	Arab conquest of Egypt, Islam becomes the main religion
c. AD 700	The Great Pyramid of Cholula, Mexico – the largest monument in the world – is completed
1798	French commander Napoleon invades Egypt, he orders a 'Description of Egypt'
1801	British forces defeat the French, and support Turkish Ottoman rule of Egypt
1882	The British Navy bombards the city of Alexandria, to secure control over the Suez Canal
1888	British archaeologist and Egyptologist William Matthew Flinders Petrie starts excavating at Hawara
1922	British archaeologist and Egyptologist Howard Carter discovers the tomb of the Pharaoh Tutankhamun
1956	Britain's direct influence over the Suez Canal ends

希腊式头盔
Greek Helmet

约公元前 7 世纪

铜合金

高 26 厘米, 宽 24.5 厘米

希腊, 遗址未知

曼彻斯特博物馆藏

　　公元前 7 世纪, 法老招募许多希腊雇佣兵以对抗外敌。这种独特的希腊式头盔可以追溯到那个时候, 它很可能是作为献给神的祭品而留在希腊神庙的。

C. 7th century BC

Copper alloy

Height 26 cm, Width 24.5 cm

Greece, site unknown

Manchester Museum

During the 7th century BC, Pharaohs employed many Greek mercenary warriors to help fight Egypt's enemies. This distinctively Greek-style helmet dates to around that time and was likely to have been left at a Greek temple as a religious gift to the gods.

2

亚述风格头盔
Assyrian Helmet

约公元前 7 世纪
铜合金
高 21 厘米, 宽 10 厘米
埃及, 底比斯
曼彻斯特博物馆藏

公元前 664 年, 亚述国王阿苏尔拔尼帕率领一支军队洗劫了埃及南部的圣城底比斯。考古学家弗林德斯 · 皮特里在底比斯 (今卢克索) 西岸发现了这种形状独特的亚述风格头盔, 并认为它可能与那场战争有一定渊源。

C. 7th century BC
Copper alloy
Height 21 cm, Width 10 cm
Egypt, Thebes
Manchester Museum

In 664 BC, an army led by the Assyrian king Ashurbanipal sacked the sacred city of Thebes in the south of Egypt. The archaeologist Flinders Petrie discovered this distinctively shaped Assyrian-style helmet on the west bank of Thebes (modern Luxor), and suggested it could date to that conflict.

3

阿尔特米多鲁斯木乃伊像
Mummy of a Man Called Artemidorus

约公元 2 世纪

镀金石膏、亚麻布和人体遗骸

高 186 厘米, 宽 53 厘米, 厚 37 厘米

埃及, 哈瓦拉

曼彻斯特博物馆藏

考古学家弗林德斯 · 皮特里认为, 这具公元 2 世纪的木乃伊是哈瓦拉一个家族墓葬的一部分。埃及风格装饰的棺木上用希腊文写有表明木乃伊主人身份的文字: "阿尔特米多鲁斯, 再会"。

C. 2nd century AD

Gilded plaster, linen and human remains

Height 186 cm, Width 53 cm, Depth 37cm

Egypt, Hawara

Manchester Museum

The archaeologist Flinders Petrie claimed that this 2nd century AD mummy was found as part of a family group at Hawara. Decorated with Egyptian funerary symbols, a Greek text identifies the deceased with the words 'Artemidorus, farewell.'

4

女性形状容器
Female-form Vessel

约公元前 1200 年
赤陶
高 25 厘米, 宽 5.4 厘米
塞浦路斯, 发现地点未知
曼彻斯特博物馆藏

在埃及发现了多种类型的塞浦路斯容器, 而在塞浦路斯岛上也有发现埃及物品的例子, 这表明至少从公元前 2000 年中期起, 两方就有了贸易往来。在塞浦路斯发现的这件容器的外形是一名埃及女性, 她戴着独特的长假发, 手上握着一只鸭子。

C.1200 BC
Terracotta
Height 25 cm, Width 5.4 cm
Cyprus, findspot unknown
Manchester Museum

A number of Cypriot vessel types have been found in Egypt, and examples of Egyptian objects found on the island of Cyprus – indicating a trade connection from at least the mid-second millennium BC. This vessel found on Cyprus takes the form of an Egyptian woman, with distinctive long wig, holding a duck.

5

动物形状容器
Animal Vessel

约公元前 7 世纪
费昂斯（主要成分为石英）
高 10.5 厘米，宽 5 厘米，厚 5 厘米
希腊，遗址未知
曼彻斯特博物馆藏

C.7th century BC
Faience
Height 10.5 cm, Width 5 cm, Depth 5cm
Greece, site unknown
Manchester Museum

约公元前 7 世纪
费昂斯(主要成分为石英)
高 5 厘米, 宽 5 厘米, 厚 6 厘米
希腊, 遗址未知
曼彻斯特博物馆藏

C.7th century BC
Faience
Height 5 cm, Width 5 cm, Depth 6cm
Greece, site unknown
Manchester Museum

动物形状容器
Animal Vessel

　　在希腊发现了许多埃及或埃及风格的物品。这些容器是为了盛放少量奢侈化妆品（例如香水）而制作的，容器的外形充满了异国情调，刺猬、狒狒和莲花图案在埃及风格的设计中很常见。

Many Egyptian or Egyptian-style objects have been found in Greece. Made to contain small amounts of luxury cosmetics like perfume, these vessels take exotic forms: hedgehogs, baboons and lotus flower motifs are common in Egyptian designs.

帕沃石碑
Stela of Pawer

约公元前 1 世纪
玄武岩
高 40.5 厘米, 宽 28.5 厘米, 厚 5 厘米
埃及, 发现地点未知
曼彻斯特博物馆藏

    石碑上半部分的图像描绘了一个名为帕沃的男子敬拜奥西里斯神和他同样为神的姐妹伊希斯和奈芙蒂斯。正文第一行使用的是古埃及通俗文字，这是有学识的埃及人日常使用的文字。其余部分是象形文字，即宗教人士使用的传统圣书体，除神职人员以外，能够识读这种文字的人寥寥无几。

C. 1st century BC
Basalt
Height 40.5 cm, Width 28.5 cm, Depth 5 cm
Egypt, findspot unknown
Manchester Museum

The upper scene shows a man named Pawer adoring the god Osiris and his divine sisters Isis and Nephthys. The first line of text is in Demotic, the everyday script of literate Egyptians, while the rest is in hieroglyphs, the traditional religious script that was understood by few outside the priesthood.

希腊文石碑
Stela with Greek Text

约公元 1 世纪

石灰岩

高 39.2 厘米, 宽 36.8 厘米, 厚 8 厘米

埃及, 发现地点未知

曼彻斯特博物馆藏

逝者的木乃伊被豺头人身的阿努比斯扶着, 进行葬礼上的"开口仪式"(使逝者在来世依旧能使用眼、耳、口、鼻);冥界统治者奥西里斯、奥西里斯的妻子伊希斯和另一个阿努比斯站在他们前面, 欢迎逝者进入来世。石碑上的希腊文祝愿逝者"再会"。

C. 1st century AD

Limestone

Height 39.2 cm, Width 36.8 cm, Depth 8 cm

Egypt, findspot unknown

Manchester Museum

The central scene shows the deceased as a mummy held up by the jackal-headed god Anubis, before Osiris, the ruler of the underworld, his wife Isis, and another figure of Anubis. Both the funeral ritual of 'Opening the Mouth' and the welcome into the afterlife are mixed. The Greek text wishes the deceased 'farewell'.

9

人像石碑
Stela of a Man

约公元 1 世纪
石灰岩
高 39 厘米, 宽 33 厘米, 厚 8 厘米
埃及, 阿拜多斯
曼彻斯特博物馆藏

　　这座石碑立于阿拜多斯城。对重生之神奥西里斯来说，这个城市是最为神圣的地方。石碑上的图像描绘了一名身着希腊服饰的男人站在两位神使之间。神使包裹着身体，豺狼的头表明他们代表的是阿努比斯神。在 "希腊 - 罗马"时期的埃及， 希腊和埃及元素的混合是这一时期的埃及多元的来世思想的典型特征。

C. 1st century AD
Limestone
Height 39 cm, Width 33 cm, Depth 8 cm
Egypt, Abydos
Manchester Museum

This stela was set up at Abydos, the site most sacred to Osiris the god of rebirth. It shows a man in Greek dress between two wrapped, divine forms; their jackal heads imply they represent the god Anubis. The mixture of Greek and Egyptian elements is typical of multicultural expectations of the afterlife in Graeco-Roman Egypt.

10

希腊文石碑
Stela with Greek Text

约公元 1 世纪

石质

高 36 厘米, 宽 56 厘米, 厚 9.5 厘米

埃及, 哈瓦拉

曼彻斯特博物馆藏

　　这块简单的石碑上, 用希腊文写着对一位逝者的致意:
"狄俄尼沙林, 卒年 45 岁。哦, 善良之人, 愿你欢心愉悦!"
这是哈瓦拉现存极少的墓志铭之一, 那里大多数墓葬都无
法确定墓主人身份。

C. 1st century AD

Stone

Height 36 cm, Width 56 cm, Depth 9.5 cm

Egypt, Hawara

Manchester Museum

This simple stela has a salutation in Greek to a deceased man:
'Dionysarin, aged 45. Oh, kindly one, be of good cheer!' This
is one of very few remains of monumental inscriptions or
grave markers from Hawara, where most burials seem to have
gone unidentified.

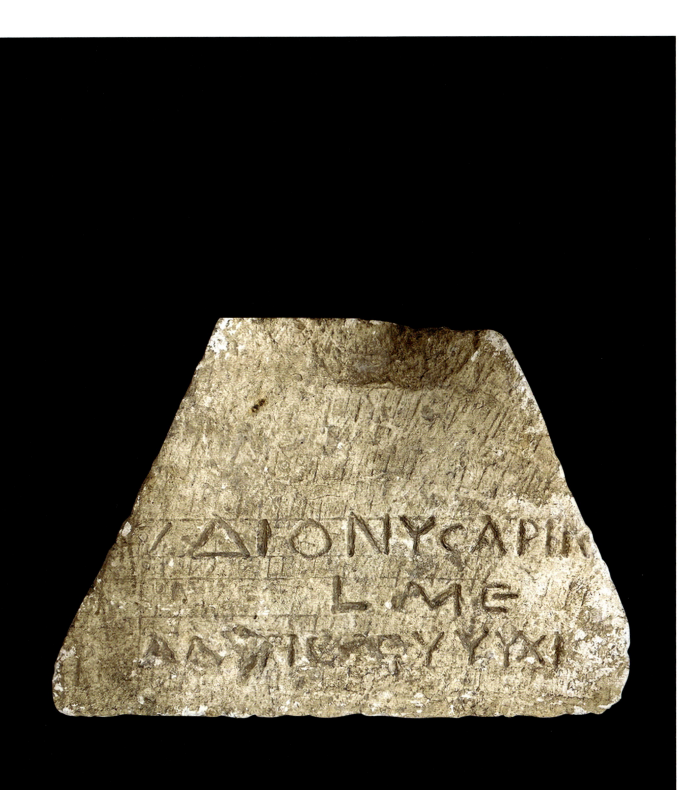

II

记录贩卖奴隶女孩的莎草纸
Sale of a Slave Girl

公元 3 世纪

莎草纸

高 27 厘米

埃及, 俄克喜林库斯

曼彻斯特博物馆藏

　　这段希腊文记录了一位富有的女性以 5 塔兰特 5000 德拉克马的价格买下了一个 12 岁的叙利亚女孩, 女孩名叫佐内娜 (在希腊语中为"佐伊")。这场于公元 282 ～ 283 年成交的交易表明, 在整个罗马帝国跨地区奴隶贸易很活跃。

3rd century AD

Papyrus

Height 27 cm

Egypt, Oxyrhynchus

Manchester Museum

This Greek text documents a wealthy woman's purchase of a 12-year-old Syrian slave girl called Zonena ('Zoe' in Greek) for the price of 5 talents and 5000 drachmas. The sale was concluded in AD 282–3 and illustrates the trans-regional slave trade active throughout the Roman Empire.

葡萄酒生产税收收据
Tax Receipt for Wine Production

约公元前 2 世纪

陶质

高 10.1 厘米, 宽 8.8 厘米

埃及, 底比斯

曼彻斯特博物馆藏

　　这块可重复使用的陶片相当于古代的便条纸，上面有由墨水写成的古埃及通俗文字，其年代可追溯至公元前102 年的埃及女王克里奥帕特拉三世和托勒密十世的统治时期。它记录了卡纳克神庙（今卢克索）附近的土地纳税情况以及那里的葡萄酒生产情况。

C. 2nd century BC

Pottery

Height 10.1 cm, Width 8.8 cm

Egypt, Thebes

Manchester Museum

This ostracon – the ancient equivalent of scrap paper – is a reused piece of potsherd with inked notation in Demotic script dated to 102 BC, in the reign of Queen Cleopatra III and King Ptolemy X. It records the tax paid on land near the temple complex of Karnak (modern Luxor) and the production of wine there.

13

记录有遗嘱内容的莎草纸
A Will

约公元 1 世纪

莎草纸

高 21.6 厘米, 宽 17.6 厘米

埃及, 俄克喜林库斯

曼彻斯特博物馆藏

遗嘱是古埃及"幸存"下来的最常见文件类型之一,它是一种规定财产从一个人向另一个人转移的法律文件。这张希腊莎草纸记载着伊施里翁之子普卢托因的部分遗嘱。

C. 1st century AD

Papyrus

Height 21.6 cm, Width 17.6 cm

Egypt, Oxyrhynchus

Manchester Museum

One of the most common types of documents to survive from Egypt in antiquity are wills – the legal document governing the transfer of property from one individual to another. This Greek papyrus carries part of the will of Plution, son of Ischyrion.

4

14

书写板
Writing Board

约公元 1 世纪
木质
高 7.5 厘米, 宽 14.5 厘米
埃及, 俄克喜林库斯
曼彻斯特博物馆藏

C. 1 century AD
Wood
Height 7.5 cm, Width 14.5 cm
Egypt, Oxyrhynchus
Manchester Museum

15

书写板
Writing Board

约公元 1 世纪
木质
高 6.8 厘米 , 宽 9.4 厘米
埃及, 俄克喜林库斯
曼彻斯特博物馆藏

C. 1st century AD
Wood
Height 6.8cm, Width 9.4 cm
Egypt, Oxyrhynchus
Manchester Museum

     这些小木板有浅凹槽用于放蜡, 蜡可以被尖笔或芦苇笔刻画, 也很容易被修改或擦拭干净。它们可能用于练习写字或传达信息, 就像一块木乃伊保护盖板残片所反映的那样。

These small tablets have a shallow depression for wax, which could be etched with a stylus or pen and easily corrected or wiped clean. They may have been used for writing practice or for carrying messages, as remains of the fixing of a protective cover suggest.

16

帝国资金使用备忘录
Memo on Imperial Funds

约公元 184 年

莎草纸

高 34.4 厘米, 宽 18 厘米

埃及, 俄克喜林库斯

曼彻斯特博物馆藏

这张莎草纸上是一份用希腊文写就的备忘录, 内容是关于帝国资金的使用情况。虽然一般认为当时的罗马皇帝康茂德并未访问过埃及, 但人们还是对这位皇帝如何使用资金非常感兴趣。

C.184 AD

Papyrus

Height 34.4 cm, Width 18 cm

Egypt, Oxyrhynchus

Manchester Museum

This papyrus sheet carries a memorandum, written in Greek script and dated to around AD 184, regarding the use of imperial funds. Although the Roman Emperor at the time – Commodus – is not believed to have visited Egypt, there was keen interest in how funds from the Emperor were used.

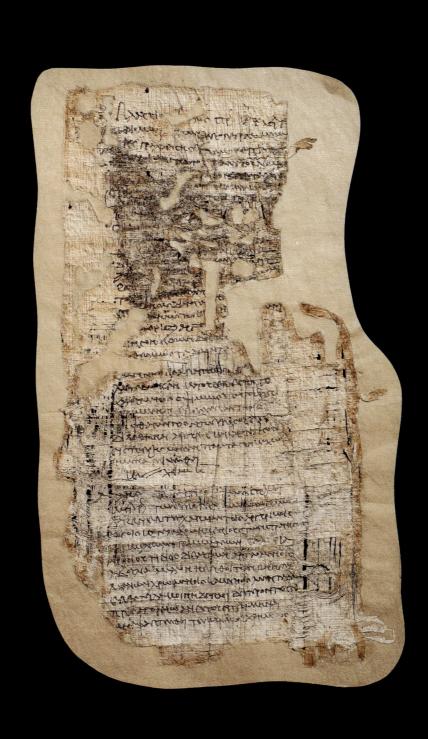

17

记录有服务契约的莎草纸
Contract for Services

约公元 8 ～ 9 年
莎草纸
高 11.7 厘米, 宽 13 厘米
埃及, 俄克喜林库斯
曼彻斯特博物馆藏

　　在"希腊 - 罗马"时期的埃及, 为某些服务订立的契约是另一种常见文件类型。这份用希腊文记录的契约可以追溯到公元 8 ～ 9 年左右。由于它的保存状况相对较差, 现在已经很难了解契约的具体内容。

C. 8-9 AD
Papyrus
Height 11.7 cm, Width 13 cm
Egypt, Oxyrhynchus
Manchester Museum

Another common type of document from Graeco-Roman Egypt are contracts for certain services. This example is written in Greek and dates to around AD 8–9. As it has been relatively poorly preserved little can be said about the nature of the transaction.

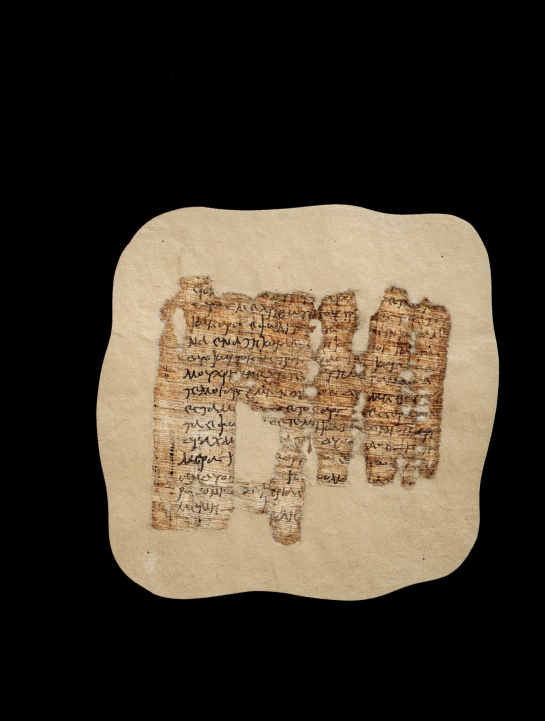

公共浴室税收收据
Tax Receipt for Public Baths

约公元 1 世纪

莎草纸

高 8 厘米, 宽 8.3 厘米

埃及, 俄克喜林库斯

曼彻斯特博物馆藏

　　在希腊人聚居区（比如在发现这件莎草纸的俄克喜林库斯），公共浴室是富裕阶层的重要社交中心。这份希腊文文件记录了浴室所有者应缴纳的税款。

C. 1st century AD

Papyrus

Height 8 cm, Width 8.3 cm

Egypt, Oxyrhynchus

Manchester Museum

Public baths were an important social hub for the wealthy in Greek settlements, such as Oxyrhynchus where this papyrus was found. This Greek text records tax to be paid by the owner of such an institution.

书吏笔盒
Scribal Palette

约公元前 1 世纪

木质

宽 38.7 厘米, 厚 5 厘米

埃及, 萨卡拉

曼彻斯特博物馆藏

这类笔盒是当时人们拥有识字能力的标志, 也是"书吏"象形文字的一部分。它用来装写字用的细芦苇笔和墨水颜料块。这个笔盒上用埃及通俗文字铭刻了所有者的姓名和头衔。

C. 1st century BC

Wood

Width 38.7cm, Depth 5cm

Egypt, Saqqara

Manchester Museum

A marker of literacy – and part of the hieroglyphic symbol of 'scribe' – was a palette such as this. It holds thin reed pens used for writing and cakes of pigment for ink. This example is inscribed in Demotic with the name and title of the owner.

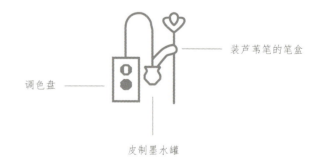

埃及象形文字"书吏"

约公元 1 世纪
玻璃
高 7 厘米, 宽 7 厘米
埃及, 萨夫特罕纳
曼彻斯特博物馆藏

C. 1st century AD
Glass
Height 7 cm, Width 7 cm
Egypt, Saft el-Henna
Manchester Museum

20

容器
Vessel

21

容器
Vessel

约公元 1 世纪
玻璃
高 20.5 厘米, 宽 13 厘米
埃及, 萨夫特罕纳
曼彻斯特博物馆藏

C. 1st century AD
Glass
Height 20.5 cm, Width 13 cm
Egypt, Saft el-Henna
Manchester Museum

约公元 1 世纪
玻璃
高 16.5 厘米, 宽 6 厘米
埃及, 哈瓦拉
曼彻斯特博物馆藏

C. 1st century AD
Glass
Height 16.5 cm, Width 6 cm
Egypt, Hawara
Manchester Museum

22

容器
Vessel

23

容器
Vessel

约公元 1 世纪
玻璃
高 16.3 厘米, 宽 3.3 厘米
埃及, 哈瓦拉
曼彻斯特博物馆藏

C. 1st century AD
Glass
Height 16.3 cm, Width 3.3 cm
Egypt, Hawara
Manchester Museum

　　绿色或浅蓝色玻璃是罗马时期的埃及最有特色的产品之一，常被用来制造这样的薄壁容器。一种被称为"泡碱"的天然碳酸钠化合物，是罗马时期生产玻璃的重要材料。在制作木乃伊时，泡碱也用于净化和干燥遗体。

Green or bluish glass is one of the most distinctive products of Roman Period Egypt, used most often to create thin-walled vessels such as these. A native Egyptian sodium compound called natron – otherwise used to purify and dehydrate the corpse in mummification – was an important element in producing Roman Period glass.

24

凸透镜片
Lens

约公元 1 世纪
玻璃
高 5.3 厘米, 宽 5.3 厘米, 厚 1 厘米
埃及, 哈瓦拉
曼彻斯特博物馆藏

　　这块引人注目的由透明玻璃制成的凸透镜是考古学家
弗林德斯 · 皮特里在哈瓦拉发现的数块凸透镜之一。皮
特里推测，这块镜片并不是用于放大物体的，而是为了将
光线聚焦在某个特定点上——比如靶心。

C. 1st century AD
Glass
Height 5.3 cm, Width 5.3 cm, Depth 1 cm
Egypt, Hawara
Manchester Museum

This remarkable convex lens of clear glass is one of several
found by Flinders Petrie at Hawara. He speculated that rather
than providing magnification, it was intended to focus light on
a particular point – like a bull's eye.

约公元前 50 年
青铜
直径 2.5 厘米
发现地点未知
曼彻斯特博物馆藏

  克里奥帕特拉七世女王是古代世界最著名的君主之一。与现代人的想像相反，她的长相与演员伊丽莎白·泰勒迥然不同。这枚硬币上的女王有着希腊式的发型和高挺的鼻子。

C. 50 BC
Bronze
Diameter 2.5 cm
Findspot unknown
Manchester Museum

Queen Cleopatra VII is one of the most famous rulers of the Ancient World. Contrary to modern fantasies, she is unlikely to have looked anything like the actress Elizabeth Taylor. The queen is depicted on coins like this with a Greek-style coiffure and a prominent nose.

25

克里奥帕特拉七世硬币
Coin of Cleopatra VII

木制玩具马
Toy Horse

约公元 1 世纪
木质
高 11.5 厘米, 宽 15.7 厘米
埃及, 古罗布
曼彻斯特博物馆藏

　　虽然很难证明这些物品是现代西方意义上的儿童玩具, 但人们还是不禁将这种"带轮子的马"视为玩具。这类物品可能参考了公元前 1 世纪维吉尔在《埃涅阿斯纪》中描述的特洛伊木马。

C. 1st century AD
Wood
Height 11.5 cm, Width 15.7cm
Egypt, Gurob
Manchester Museum

While it is difficult to prove objects were used as children's toys in the modern Western sense, it is tempting to view this model horse-on-wheels as such. One of several known, such objects were perhaps made in reference to the Trojan Horse, described by Virgil in the Aeneid of the 1st century BC.

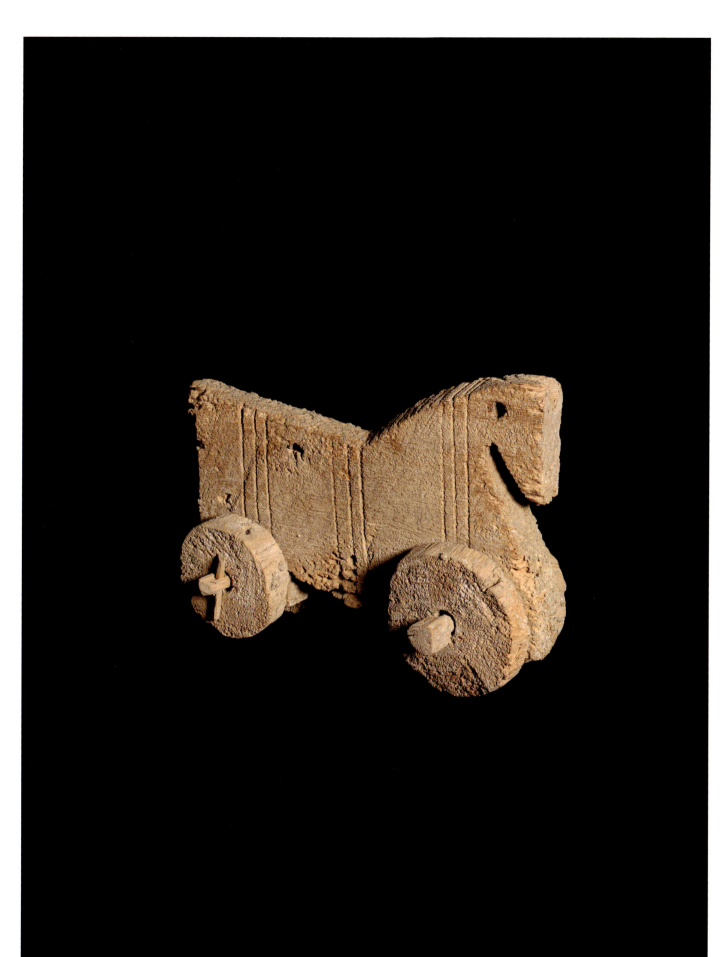

27

铙
Cymbal

约公元 1 世纪

青铜

宽 20.8 厘米, 厚 4.5 厘米

埃及, 高卡博尔

曼彻斯特博物馆藏

　　在埃及庙宇中，祭司会使用很多乐器来取悦神灵。铙作为一种打击乐器，在公元前最后几个世纪才出现在埃及。这件铙上有一个可以挤压的手柄，通过按压产生乐声。

C. 1st century AD

Bronze

Width 20.8cm, Depth 4.5cm

Egypt, Qaw el-Kabir

Manchester Museum

Musical instruments were used in Egyptian temples to entertain the gods. Cymbals as a form of percussive instrument only appeared in Egypt in the last centuries BC. This example has a handle to squeeze to make music.

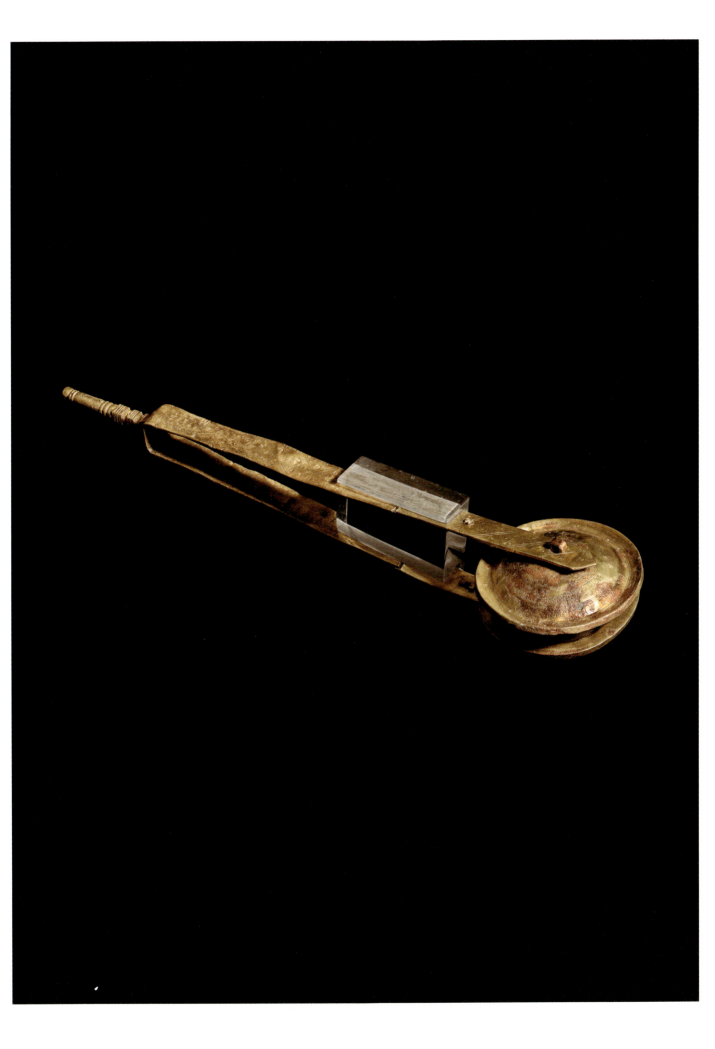

28

篮子
Basket

约公元 1 世纪
棕榈纤维
高 17.5 厘米, 宽 19.2 厘米
埃及, 俄克喜林库斯
曼彻斯特博物馆藏

  用棕榈纤维制成的篮子用途广泛, 这在古代埃及和现代埃及都很常见。埃及沙漠的干燥条件有利于保存这种常见的家庭物品。

C. 1st century AD
Palm
Height 17.5 cm, Width 19.2cm
Egypt, Oxyrhynchus
Manchester Museum

Basketry made from the split leaves of palm trees – which were and remain common in Egypt – had a number of uses. The dry conditions of Egypt's deserts have preserved this common household material.

约公元 1 世纪

陶质

高 8.2 厘米, 宽 9.5 厘米, 厚 8.5 厘米

埃及, 哈瓦拉

曼彻斯特博物馆藏

古埃及人认为熏香的芳香可以吸引神灵出现。焚香可能与神像一起组合使用，在神庙和家庭的相关仪式中都非常重要。这个香炉呈希腊式祭坛形状，因使用过而变黑。

C. 1st century AD

Pottery

Height 8.2 cm, Width 9.5 cm, Depth 8.5cm

Egypt, Hawara

Manchester Museum

The sweet fragrance of incense was thought to invite the presence of the gods. Perhaps used in conjunction with figurines of gods, burning incense was very important in temple and household ritual. This stand or burner is in the shape of a Greek-style altar and is blackened from use.

29

香炉
Incense Burner

混合的神
Hybrid Gods

　　虽然埃及神庙中神祇的样貌几乎都是传统法老时代的样式，但有大量证据表明，在"希腊-罗马"时期，古埃及人在家中敬奉的神祇种类更多。成千上万的陶质神像留存至今，它们大多发现于生活区遗址，少数发现于神庙和坟墓遗址附近。一般来说，它们的外观都偏于古希腊风格，但往往也结合了传统埃及法老时代神祇的元素。虽然这些神像上一般都没有铭文，但它们的特征使得我们可以很容易地分辨出不同的神祇。

While the gods depicted in Egyptian temples almost always adopt traditionally Pharaonic forms, there is plentiful evidence of the worship of a much wider variety of deities in peoples' homes during the Graeco-Roman Period. Many thousands of hollow terracotta figurines survive, deriving mainly from domestic contexts – although some have also been found near temples and in graves. Generally, these display a preference for a Classical appearance, but often combine Pharaonic elements. Although almost never inscribed, specific features make individual deities easy to recognise.

约公元 1 世纪

大理石

高 33 厘米, 宽 22 厘米, 厚 13.5 厘米

发现地点未知

曼彻斯特博物馆藏

　　对埃及女神伊希斯的崇拜风靡整个罗马帝国，远至现今的英国北部。这尊伊希斯半身像呈现出古希腊的风格，她的头发是典型的希腊式螺旋状卷发，而头上程式化的太阳圆盘头饰和牛角又表明她是一位埃及神祇。

C. 1st century AD

Marble

Height 33 cm, Width 22 cm, Depth 13.5cm

Findspot unknown

Manchester Museum

The cult of the Egyptian mother goddess Isis spread throughout the Roman Empire, as far north as Britain. This bust shows Isis in Classical form, with her hair in typical corkscrew curls. Her Egyptian identity is indicated by the stylized solar disk and cow's horns above her head.

50

伊希斯半身像

Bust of Isis

51

哈托尔神像
Figurine of Hathor

约公元 1 世纪
赤陶
高 26 厘米, 宽 8.5 厘米, 厚 5 厘米
发现地点未知
曼彻斯特博物馆藏

C. 1st century AD
Terracotta
Height 26 cm, Width 8.5 cm, Depth 5 cm
Findspot unknown
Manchester Museum

52

哈托尔神像
Figurine of Hathor

约公元 1 世纪

赤陶

高 23 厘米, 宽 6.5 厘米, 厚 4 厘米

发现地点未知

曼彻斯特博物馆藏

C. 1st century AD

Terracotta

Height 23 cm, Width 6.5 cm, Depth 4 cm

Findspot unknown

Manchester Museum

许多女神雕像都被塑造为这种独特外形，包括伊希斯和阿芙洛狄忒在内，但埃及女神哈托尔是其中最典型的。她代表性与重生，这种曲线优美的雕像在"希腊 - 罗马"时期的女性棺木中经常可见。

Various goddesses have been identified as being represented by this distinctive form, including Isis and Aphrodite, although the Egyptian goddess Hathor is most likely. She represented sexuality as well as rebirth, and this curvaceous form is replicated in a number of female coffins of the Graeco-Roman Period.

33

战士形象的贝斯神
Bes as a Soldier

约公元前 1 世纪
赤陶
高 35 厘米, 宽 12 厘米
埃及, 发现地点未知
曼彻斯特博物馆藏

C. 1st century BC
Terracotta
Height 35 cm, Width 12 cm
Egypt, findspot unknown
Manchester Museum

34

战士形象的贝斯神
Bes as a Soldier

约公元前 1 世纪

赤陶

高 18.5 厘米, 宽 9 厘米, 厚 4.5 厘米

埃及, 发现地点未知

曼彻斯特博物馆藏

C. 1st century BC

Terracotta

Height 18.5 cm, Width 9 cm, Depth 4.5cm

Egypt, findspot unknown

Manchester Museum

　　在埃及神话中, 贝斯勇武好战, 能驱妖除魔, 保护刚生产的产妇和幼童免受邪灵侵扰。他穿着马其顿风格的盔甲, 可以推断出这尊雕像可能制作于托勒密王朝时期。该王朝统治者来自马其顿。

The Egyptian god Bes was traditionally depicted as an aggressive being, effective at warding off evil spirits – especially from new mothers and young children. He wears Macedonian-style armour, so probably dates to the Ptolemaic Period, whose rulers' origins were in Macedon.

35

游神仪式中携带的神龛
Shrine Carried in Procession

约公元 1 世纪
赤陶
高 23.5 厘米, 宽 11 厘米
埃及, 哈瓦拉
曼彻斯特博物馆藏

　　这座雕像曾被解读为表现了一位上层阶级的女子被仆从抬上轿椅, 不过现在更有可能的解释是, 它是祭司在游行中携带的女神雕像。这种陶器可能一般出现在宗教庆典上。

C. 1st century AD
Terracotta
Height 23.5cm, Width 11 cm
Egypt, Hawara
Manchester Museum

Once believed to show an elite lady being carried by porters in a sedan chair, a more likely interpretation of this figurine is that it represents a statue of a goddess being carried in procession by priests. Production of such terracottas may have coincided with religious celebrations.

56

骑河马的哈波克拉特斯赤陶像
Harpocrates on a Hippo

约公元 1 世纪

赤陶

高 14.5 厘米, 宽 11 厘米

埃及, 发现地点未知

曼彻斯特博物馆藏

　　河马是生活在尼罗河畔的猛兽, 但它们也是埃及人心中保护弱者的强大象征。从这件雕像的外形判断, 骑在河马上的神祇可能是儿童保护神哈波克拉特斯。

C. 1st century AD

Terracotta

Height 14.5 cm, Width 11 cm

Egypt, findspot unknown

Manchester Museum

Hippopotami were fearsome animals that lived on the banks of the River Nile, yet they were also a powerful Egyptian symbol of protection for the vulnerable. The form of this figurine may allude to the child god Harpocrates as a protector.

57

宙斯神像
Figurine of Zeus

约公元 1 世纪

赤陶

高 16.5 厘米, 宽 7.9 厘米

埃及, 发现地点未知

曼彻斯特博物馆藏

    宙斯是希腊众神之王。他的经典形象启发了对塞拉皮斯形象的塑造。塞拉皮斯是托勒密王朝推崇的多元文化神,是埃及神奥西里斯和诸多希腊神祇的糅合。对塞拉皮斯的崇拜远远超出埃及,遍布整个罗马帝国。

C. 1st century AD

Terracotta

Height 16.5 cm, Width 7.9 cm

Egypt, findspot unknown

Manchester Museum

Zeus was the king of the Greek gods. His Classical appearance inspired depictions of Serapis, a multicultural god promoted by the Ptolemies, combining the Egyptian god Osiris with a number of Hellenistic deities. Worship of Serapis travelled far outside Egypt's borders, throughout the Roman Empire.

58

骑鹅的哈波克拉特斯赤陶像
Harpocrates on a Goose

约公元 1 世纪

赤陶

高 15.2 厘米, 宽 7.5 厘米

埃及, 发现地点未知

曼彻斯特博物馆藏

　　鹅是底比斯阿蒙神的圣兽之一。但鹅在这件雕像中的意义尚未完全弄清。"手托一只罐子的哈波克拉特斯"是常见的装饰主题, 不过这个主题的意义尚未明确。

C. 1st century AD

Terracotta

Height 15.2 cm, Width 7.5 cm

Egypt, findspot unknown

Manchester Museum

Geese were one of the sacred animals of the Theban god Amun, although the significance of the bird here is not entirely clear. Harpocrates has his hand in a pot, which is a common motif – although of uncertain meaning.

39

戴双王冠的哈波克拉特斯赤陶像
Harpocrates with a Double Crown

约公元 1 世纪

赤陶

高 24.2 厘米, 宽 18.3 厘米

埃及, 发现地点未知

曼彻斯特博物馆藏

    在"希腊-罗马"时期, 哈波克拉特斯的身份是孩提时的埃及神荷鲁斯, 他一般头戴象征统一埃及的双王冠。"哈波克拉特斯左手持罐"这个主题的意义尚未明确。

C. 1st century AD

Terracotta

Height 24.2cm, Width 18.3 cm

Egypt, findspot unknown

Manchester Museum

Harpocrates was a Graeco-Roman version of the Egyptian god Horus-the-Child, who traditionally wore the double crown of a united Egypt. Here the god holds a jar in his left hand, a motif of uncertain significance.

40

骑马的哈波克拉特斯赤陶像
Harpocrates on Horseback

约公元 1 世纪

赤陶

高 13.9 厘米, 宽 8.9 厘米

埃及, 发现地点未知

曼彻斯特博物馆藏

　　儿童保护神哈波克拉特斯骑着一匹疾驰的马, 戴着缩小版的埃及双王冠。这件小雕像的外形可能与他平息混乱或排除危险的主题相呼应, 在这里以他饲养的马来表达这种寓意。

C. 1st century AD

Terracotta

Height 13.9 cm, Width 8.9 cm

Egypt, findspot unknown

Manchester Museum

The child god Harpocrates rides a galloping horse and wears a miniature version of the double crown of Egypt. The form of this figurine may echo an earlier motif of the infant god pacifying chaos or danger, represented here by the rearing stallion.

德墨忒耳小雕像
Figurine of Demeter

约公元 1 世纪

赤陶

高 22.2 厘米, 宽 7 厘米

埃及, 发现地点未知

曼彻斯特博物馆藏

　　手执长火炬是希腊女神德墨忒耳的重要标识。对希腊人来说，德墨忒耳是专司农业和丰收的女神，这位神祇很适合埃及这样的农业社会，尤其是法尤姆这样土地肥沃的地区。

C. 1st century AD

Terracotta

Height 22.2 cm, Width 7cm

Egypt, findspot unknown

Manchester Museum

The Greek goddess Demeter is identifiable by the long torch she holds. For the Greeks, Demeter was the goddess of the harvest and agriculture, a deity appropriate for an agrarian society such as that of Egypt, especially as sites like those in the fertile Faiyum area.

约公元 1 世纪

铜合金

高 21.5 厘米, 宽 6.5 厘米

埃及, 发现地点未知

曼彻斯特博物馆藏

　　这尊古典风格雕像上的羽冠表明她是伊希斯 - 阿芙洛狄忒女神。在公元前最后几个世纪, 伊希斯越来越多地佩戴上了哈托尔的牛角头饰, 这两位埃及女神在某种意义上变得难以区分。阿芙洛狄忒是希腊的爱情女神, 与哈托尔和伊希斯都有一定联系。

C. 1st century AD

Copper alloy

Height 21.5 cm, Width 6.5 cm

Egypt, findspot unknown

Manchester Museum

The plumed crown marks this otherwise Classical figurine as a representation of the goddess Isis-Aphrodite. Increasingly in the last centuries BC, Isis took on the cow-horned headdress of Hathor and these two Egyptian goddesses in some sense became indistinguishable. Aphrodite was the Greek goddess of love and associated with both Hathor and Isis.

42

伊希斯－阿芙洛狄忒雕像
Figurine of Isis-Aphrodite

43

香炉
Incense Burner

约公元 1 世纪
赤陶
高 15.5 厘米, 宽 10 厘米
埃及, 发现地点未知
曼彻斯特博物馆藏

　　香炉是在神庙或者家中神龛使用的香具，炉上的孔让芳香的烟雾萦绕整个空间。这尊香炉的表面使用了一种独特的黏土装饰技术——"巴尔博汀（装饰用料浆）"，这是某些类型麦罗埃陶器的典型特征。

C. 1st century AD
Terracotta
Height 15.5 cm, Width 10 cm
Egypt, findspot unknown
Manchester Museum

This perforated vessel allowed the fragrant smoke of burning incense to fumigate a sacred or domestic space. The distinctive technique of applied clay decoration – called 'barbotine' – is typical of some types of Meroitic ceramics.

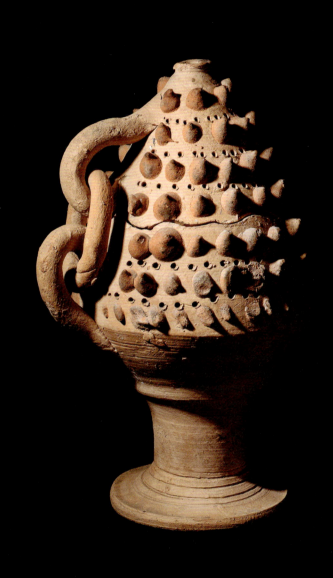

麦罗埃王国
The Kingdom of Meroe

　　麦罗埃王国因其主要城市麦罗埃而得名，这座城市位于今天的苏丹喀土穆以北约200公里（125英里）。麦罗埃王国与埃及的希腊-罗马时期同期存在（公元前300～公元350年）。麦罗埃文化有自己的文字，大部分仍未被破译，其统治者也建造了很多金字塔，数量上比埃及现存的金字塔还要多。装饰独特的陶器是麦罗埃文化中最有标志性的物品之一。公元前21年-公元前20年，在"麦罗埃-罗马战争"之后，麦罗埃王国和埃及之间重新建立了大规模的贸易联系。

The Kingdom of Meroe takes its name from its principal city of Meroe some 200km (125 miles) north of Khartoum in present-day Sudan and existed at the same time as the Ptolemaic and Roman Period in Egypt (c. 300 BC–AD 350). Meroitic culture had its own script, which remains largely undeciphered, and built more pyramids for its rulers than are presently standing in Egypt. One of the culture's most recognizable products is its distinctively decorated pottery. Large-scale trading contacts were re-established between the Meroitic Kingdom and Egypt in 21/20 BC after the Meroitic-Roman War.

44

麦罗埃陶罐

Meroitic Vessel

约公元 1 世纪

陶质

高 13.1 厘米, 宽 15.7 厘米

苏丹, 法拉斯

曼彻斯特博物馆藏

C. 1st century AD

Pottery

Height 13.1 cm, Width 15.7 cm

Sudan, Faras

Manchester Museum

麦罗埃陶器以独特且大胆的设计而闻名，它通常融合了莲花、蛇或风格化的"安可"（生命之符）符号等各种埃及图案。这些陶罐证明了在"希腊 - 罗马"时期埃及与南部邻邦之间的文化交流。

Recognisable by their distinctive bold designs, Meroitic pottery often incorporates Egyptian motifs like lotus flowers, serpents or stylized ankh ('life') symbols. These vessels attest to the cultural contacts between Egypt and its southern neighbours during the Graeco-Roman Period.

麦罗埃陶罐
Meroitic Vessel

约公元 1 世纪
陶质
高 9.7 厘米, 宽 9 厘米
苏丹, 法拉斯
曼彻斯特博物馆藏

C. 1st century AD
Pottery
Height 9.7 cm, Width 9 cm
Sudan, Faras
Manchester Museum

麦罗埃陶罐
Meroitic Vessel

约公元 1 世纪
陶质
高 22 厘米, 宽 20.9 厘米
苏丹, 法拉斯
曼彻斯特博物馆藏

C. 1st century AD
Pottery
Height 22 cm, Width 20.9 cm
Sudan, Faras
Manchester Museum

约公元 1 世纪
陶质
高 4.9 厘米, 宽 10.1 厘米
苏丹, 法拉斯
曼彻斯特博物馆藏

C. 1st century AD
Pottery
Height 4.9 cm, Width 10.1 cm
Sudan, Faras
Manchester Museum

47

麦罗埃陶碗
Meroitic Bowl

48

麦罗埃陶罐
Meroitic Vessel

约公元 1 世纪
陶质
高 7.2 厘米, 宽 9.5 厘米
苏丹, 法拉斯
曼彻斯特博物馆藏

C. 1st century AD
Pottery
Height 7.2cm, Width 9.5 cm
Sudan, Faras
Manchester Museum

49

麦罗埃陶罐
Meroitic Vessel

约公元 1 世纪
陶质
高 6.4 厘米, 宽 8.8 厘米
苏丹, 法拉斯
曼彻斯特博物馆藏

C. 1st century AD
Pottery
Height 6.4 cm, Width 8.8 cm
Sudan, Faras
Manchester Museum

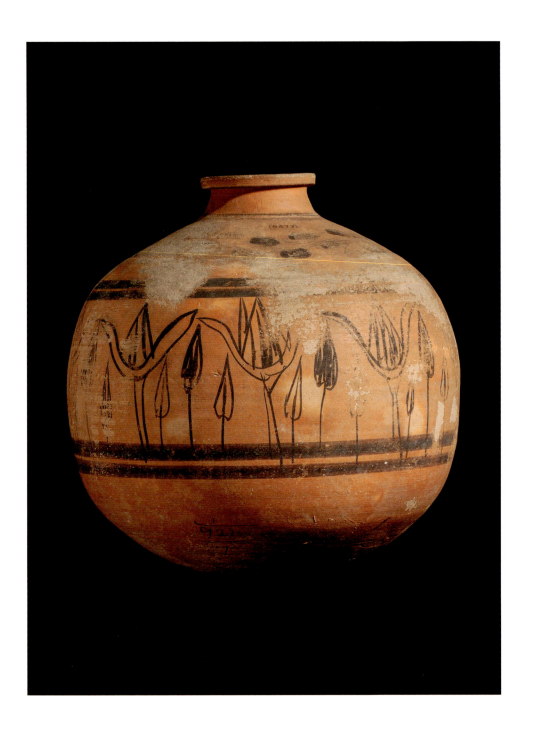

50

麦罗埃陶罐
Meroitic Vessel

约公元 1 世纪
陶质
高 28.5 厘米, 宽 28.5 厘米
苏丹, 法拉斯
曼彻斯特博物馆藏

C. 1st century AD
Pottery
Height 28.5cm, Width 28.5 cm
Sudan, Faras
Manchester Museum

5I

麦罗埃陶罐
Meroitic Vessel

约公元 1 世纪
陶质
高 7.8 厘米, 宽 8.7 厘米
苏丹, 法拉斯
曼彻斯特博物馆藏

C. 1st century AD
Pottery
Height 7.8 cm, Width 8.7 cm
Sudan, Faras
Manchester Museum

52

脚镯
Pair of Anklets

约公元 3 世纪

铜质

高 4 厘米, 宽 11.5 厘米

苏丹, 法拉斯

曼彻斯特博物馆藏

　　麦罗埃王国以卓越的金属加工技术而闻名, 珠宝是王国与罗马帝国开展贸易活动的重要商品。这些笨重的珠宝都是在墓葬中发现的, 制造时间可以追溯到公元 3 世纪左右。

C. 3rd century AD

Copper

Height 4 cm, Width 11.5 cm

Sudan, Faras

Manchester Museum

The Meroitic kingdom was well-known for exceptionally fine metal working, and this provided an important trade connection with the Roman Empire. These heavy pieces of jewellery were found in graves and date to around the 3rd century AD.

来世思想
Ideas about the Afterlife

在"希腊-罗马"时期，对死亡和来世的准备工作受到了埃及、希腊和罗马传统的影响。希腊人和罗马人对他们死后的存在抱有相当悲观的期望。然而，埃及人的来世观念为他们提供了重生到一个光明且完美世界的可能性，人们加入到崇拜重生之神和冥界统治者奥西里斯的行列里，并相信能得以永生。

葬礼是展示财富和地位的重要机会。棺木、面具和木乃伊的装饰都是鲜亮夺目的，用的都是只有富人才能买得起的昂贵材料。这些物品显示逝者在重生的那一刻是活着且清醒的——这种神奇的情景被人们所确信。逝去的人们被描绘成自己的完美形象，即使是那些在童年时期死去的人看起来也好像已经长大了，这样他们就能最大限度地享受来世。

During the Graeco-Roman Period, preparations for death and the afterlife were influenced by Egyptian, Greek and Roman traditions. Greeks and Romans had rather bleak expectations for an existence after death. However, the Egyptian afterlife offered them the possibility of being reborn into a bright, perfected version of this world, to join Osiris, the god of rebirth and ruler of the Underworld, and to live on for eternity.

The funeral was an important opportunity to display wealth and status. Coffins, masks and mummy decorations were bright and eye-catching, involving costly materials for the wealthy. These show the deceased as alive and awake, at the moment of rebirth – magically assuring that this would be the case. People are depicted as perfect versions of themselves; even those who died as children appear as if they had grown up, so they could enjoy the afterlife to the fullest.

永生的保护
Armoured for Eternity

    几个世纪以来，埃及上层阶级在死后都被放入木棺埋葬，但在"希腊-罗马"时期，这种木棺基本已经不再使用。取而代之的是，木乃伊有时会被盖上面具并蒙上其他盖板，用亚麻绷带固定。面具和盖板由制造木乃伊棺的材料制成——亚麻或莎草纸和石膏的混合物，类似混凝纸浆。面具或盖板的表面也经过装饰，旨在借助神力保护逝者。最重要的是，木乃伊面具被认为能让逝者在来世拥有视力。这种面具通常使用模具制造，能大批量生产。它们描绘出逝者完美的、神一般的面孔，而不是现代西方意义上的肖像。

For centuries the Egyptian elite had been buried in wooden coffins – but these largely fell out of use in the Graeco-Roman Period. Instead, the mummy was sometimes provided with a mask and other coverings attached with the outer linen bandages. These elements are made of cartonnage – a mixture of linen or papyrus and plaster, similar to papier-mâché – and provided surfaces for decoration designed to magically protect the deceased. Most importantly, the mummy mask was believed to allow the deceased the power of sight in the afterlife. Such masks were mass produced, and often mould made. They depict the deceased with the perfect face of a god-like being and were not intended to be portraits in the modern Western sense.

"重要的木乃伊被放在我的床下。"

——考古学家威廉·马修·弗林德斯·皮特里，1931 年

"Important mummies were put under my bed"

William Matthew Flinders Petrie, archaeologist, 1931

约公元前 1 世纪

镀金、彩绘石膏和亚麻布

高 128 厘米, 宽 58 厘米, 厚 36 厘米

埃及, 阿赫米姆

曼彻斯特博物馆藏

这个石膏和亚麻布盖板是用来盖在一个无名女孩的木乃伊上的。她身着希腊风格的服装，佩戴着成人的首饰。精致的花卉头饰和成年人曲线优美的身体比例让人想起当时的哈托尔女神雕像。这种风格表明这副盖板可能制作于公元前 1 世纪。

C. 1st century BC

Gilded, painted plaster and linen

Height 128cm, Width 58cm, Depth 36cm

Egypt, Akhmim

Manchester Museum

This moulded plaster and linen cover was made to be placed over the mummy of an unnamed girl. She wears Greek-style dress and jewellery normally worn by an adult. The elaborate floral headpiece and curvaceous adult body proportions evoke contemporary figurines of the goddess Hathor. The style suggests a date of the 1st century BC.

53

年轻女孩的木乃伊盖板
Mummy Cover for a Young Girl

54

年轻女孩的木乃伊裹尸布
Mummy Shroud of a Young Girl

约公元 1 世纪
镀金、亚麻布
高 122 厘米, 宽 40 厘米, 厚 1 厘米
埃及, 安提诺
曼彻斯特博物馆藏

　　在古埃及, 幼童多早殇。裹尸布上描绘的这位年轻女
孩手拿花环, 右手举起, 手掌朝外, 摆出问候或祈祷的姿
势。她被埃及众神包围, 仿佛自神龛而出——暗示着逝者
的神性。

C. 1st century AD
Gilded, linen
Height 122 cm, Width 40 cm, Depth 1 cm
Egypt, Antinoe
Manchester Museum

Many young children did not live into adulthood. This young
girl holds a floral garland, and her right hand is raised, palm
outwards, in a gesture of greeting or prayer. Her figure is
framed by scenes of Egyptian gods, within a Pharaonic
gateway as if emerging from a shrine – suggesting the divine
nature of the deceased.

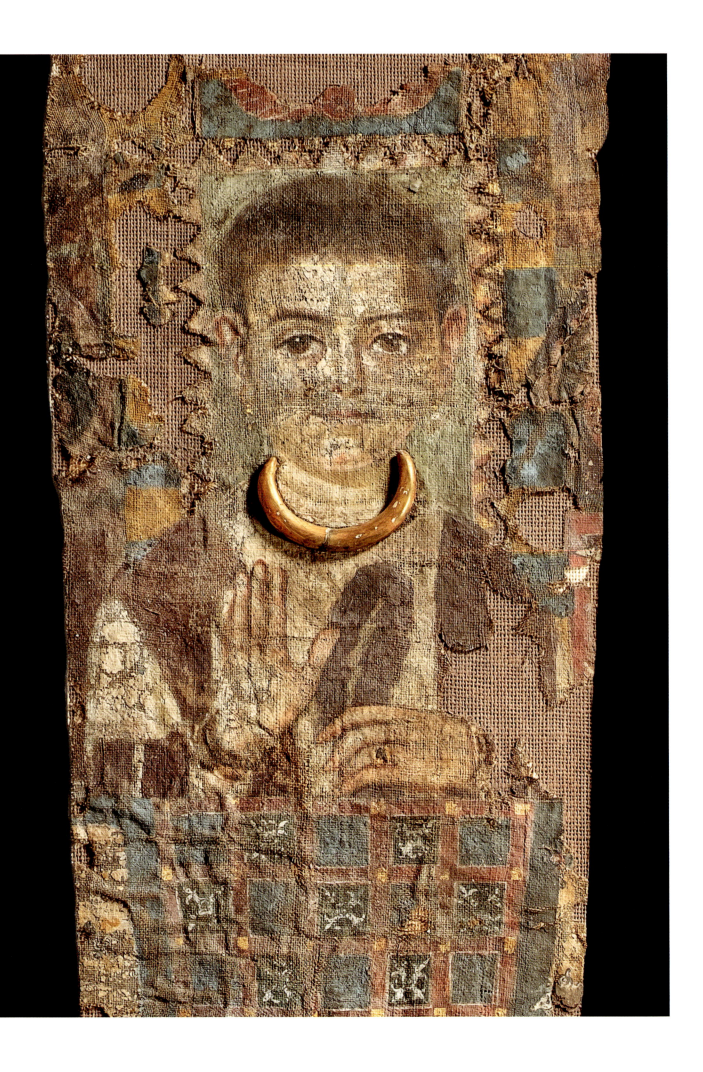

55

木乃伊胸部盖板
Mummy Chest Cover

约公元前 1 世纪
彩绘石膏
高 47.5 厘米, 宽 28.2 厘米, 厚 9 厘米
埃及, 哈瓦拉
曼彻斯特博物馆藏

　　这件胸部盖板上的人头圣甲虫装饰，据说能为逝者的心脏提供神奇的保护。线条是木乃伊上被移除的亚麻布条留下的痕迹，这些亚麻布条起着固定木乃伊的作用。写在盖板背面的一段通俗埃及文字提到了木乃伊主人的名字。

C. 1st century BC
Painted plaster
Height 47.5 cm, Width 28.2cm, Depth 9 cm
Egypt, Hawara
Manchester Museum

Decorated with a human-headed scarab, this chest cover provided magical protection for the heart of the deceased. Lines show where the mummy's linen wrappings, once used to hold the piece in place, have been removed. A short note written in Demotic script on the reverse gives the name of the owner.

56

木乃伊面具
Mummy Mask

约公元前 1 世纪

彩绘石膏

高 46.5 厘米, 宽 28 厘米, 厚 15 厘米

埃及, 哈瓦拉

曼彻斯特博物馆藏

　　这副使用模具、由亚麻布和石膏制成的面具, 是托勒密王朝时期和罗马时期法尤姆地区的典型风格。面具头部的彩绘模仿了青金石的蓝色, 青金石被认为是埃及神祇的头发, 这样可以将逝者与神明联系在一起。

C. 1st century BC

Painted plaster

Height 46.5 cm, Width 28 cm, Depth 15 cm

Egypt, Hawara

Manchester Museum

This is one of a series of mould-made masks, built up from layers of linen and plaster, typical of the Faiyum region during the Ptolemaic and Roman Periods. The distinctive blue colour of the head covering is in emulation of the lapis lazuli believed to be the hair of Egyptian deities, thus associating the deceased with the divine.

57

木乃伊胸部盖板
Mummy Chest Cover

约公元前 1 世纪
彩绘石膏和亚麻布
高 37.5 厘米, 宽 20.2 厘米, 厚 10 厘米
埃及, 哈瓦拉
曼彻斯特博物馆藏

　　这件有装饰的木乃伊盖板上有象形文字题词, 从中可以得知逝者的名字为"尼玛特"——这是阿蒙涅姆赫特三世的名字之一。阿蒙涅姆赫特三世是一位被尊为神祇的哈瓦拉法老, 他生活在这件木乃伊胸部盖板的主人出生前约 1500 年的时代。

C. 1st century BC
Painted plaster and linen
Height 37.5 cm, Width 20.2cm, Depth 10 cm
Egypt, Hawara
Manchester Museum

The hieroglyphic inscription on this decorated piece of cartonnage (similar to papier-mâché) names the deceased as 'Nimaatre', one of the names of Amenemhat III, a king venerated as a god at Hawara and who lived around 1500 years before the owner of this object was born.

58

女性木乃伊面具
Mummy Mask of a Woman

约公元 1 世纪

彩绘石膏

高 57 厘米, 宽 28 厘米, 厚 15 厘米

埃及, 梅尔

曼彻斯特博物馆藏

　　这副面具的设计——镀金的细节和玻璃制成的眼睛, 与在埃及中部梅尔遗址发现的一组面具几乎相同, 表明它可能来自那一地区。这一地区的其他面具后侧有很长的突出部分, 用以覆盖木乃伊的头部, 且通常绘有彩色埃及神祇图。

C. 1st century AD

Painted plaster

Height 57 cm, Width 28 cm, Depth 15 cm

Egypt, Meir

Manchester Museum

The design of this mask, with gilded details and the eyes added in glass, indicate that it came from a group of near-identical masks found at the site of Meir in Middle Egypt. Other examples have deep side projections to cover the head that often carry colourful scenes of Egyptian gods.

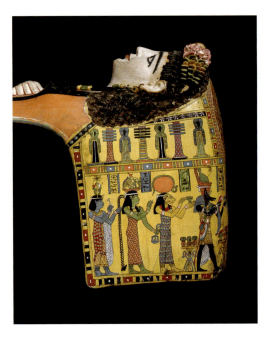

木乃伊面具, 公元 1 世纪, 大都会博物馆藏

59

木乃伊面具
Mummy Mask

约公元 1 世纪
彩绘石膏
高 22.5 厘米, 宽 16 厘米, 厚 20 厘米
埃及, 迈莱维
曼彻斯特博物馆藏

C. 1st century AD
Painted plaster
Height 22.5 cm, Width 16 cm, Depth 20 cm
Egypt, Mallawi
Manchester Museum

约公元 1 世纪

彩绘石膏

高 20 厘米, 宽 17 厘米, 厚 22 厘米

埃及, 迈莱维

曼彻斯特博物馆藏

C. 1st century AD

Painted plaster

Height 20 cm, Width 17 cm, Depth 22cm

Egypt, Mallawi

Manchester Museum

木乃伊面具

Mummy Mask

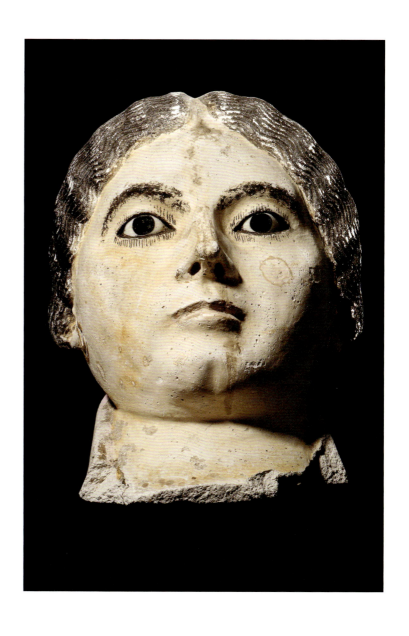

木乃伊面具
Mummy Mask

约公元 1 世纪
彩绘石膏
高 24 厘米, 宽 17 厘米, 厚 12 厘米
埃及, 迈莱维
曼彻斯特博物馆藏

　　这些石膏"头部"被固定在棺盖上或直接固定在木乃伊上, 让逝者看起来如同醒着一般。像木乃伊彩绘画像一样, 他们的发型和饰品都各不相同。石膏头部很容易与主体分离, 因此经常被出售于艺术市场。

C. 1st century AD
Painted plaster
Height 24 cm, Width 17 cm, Depth 12 cm
Egypt, Mallawi
Manchester Museum

These plaster heads were attached to coffin lids or fixed directly onto mummies and show the deceased as if awakened. Like the painted portraits, they display different fashions in hairstyles and jewellery. These were easily detached and often sold on the art market.

62

女性木乃伊面具
Mummy Mask of a Woman

约公元 1 世纪

彩绘石膏

高 44 厘米, 宽 25 厘米, 厚 16 厘米

埃及, 发现地点未知

曼彻斯特博物馆藏

　　这副面具上仍然保留了很多最初的颜色, 她有黑色的头发, 穿着紫色条纹外套。衣服两边的直角白色条纹末端有凹口, 是织工的记号。

C. 1st century AD

Painted plaster

Height 44 cm, Width 25 cm, Depth 16 cm

Egypt, findspot unknown

Manchester Museum

This mask still retains much of its original paint colouring, with a black hair and purple striped garment. Weaver's marks on each side of this cloth are shown as white stripes at a right angle and notched at the ends.

63

伊希斯和奥西里斯
Isis and Osiris

约公元 1 世纪

木质

高 31.5 厘米

埃及, 图纳盖贝勒

曼彻斯特博物馆藏

　　这块镂雕木板描绘女神伊希斯展开翅膀, 以保护她的丈夫——重生之神奥西里斯。木板上方的象形文字拼出了他的名字。这件不知出处的物品所表现出的独特艺术风格与中埃及的图纳盖贝勒的同类物品相似, 据此推测它或许来自那一地区。

C. 1st century AD

Wood

Height 31.5 cm

Egypt, Tuna el-Gebel

Manchester Museum

This openwork panel shows the goddess Isis stretching her wings protectively behind her husband Osiris, the god of rebirth. Hieroglyphs spell out his name. The distinctive artistic style resembles those from Tuna el-Gebel in Middle Egypt, suggesting an origin for this unprovenanced piece.

成为神
Becoming a God

Ⅲ

在埃及的传统中，诸神是不朽的。为了在众神中获得永恒的存在，逝者在某种意义上要成为其中一员。死去的男女可以与重生之神奥西里斯合而为一，到了"希腊 - 罗马"时代，逝去的女性可以与西方女神哈托尔融合。

为了达到这一目的，逝者遗体必须在仪式上进行处理，只有贵族才有条件完全遵循繁复的步骤。木乃伊外观模仿了古埃及神的样子，据说神有不会变色的黄金肉身和珍贵的青金石头发，所以那些能负担得起的贵族通常备有棺木、面具或其他装饰着金箔的覆盖物，头罩被涂成蓝色。拥有这种神圣意象的保护是获得永生的最好方式。

In Egyptian tradition, the gods were immortal. In order to attain an eternal presence among the gods the deceased had, in some sense, to become one. Dead men and women could become one with Osiris, the god of rebirth, and by Graeco-Roman times deceased women could merge with Hathor, the Mistress of the West – where the sun set.

In order to achieve this goal, the body of the deceased had to undergo special ritual preparations available in their fullest only to the wealthy. The creation and appearance of a wrapped mummy replicated the ancient form of an Egyptian god. Egyptian deities were said to have flesh of untarnishable gold and hair of semi-precious lapis lazuli stone, so those who could afford it often had a coffin, mask or other covering decorated with gold leaf with a head covering painted in blue. Being armed with this divine imagery was the best means of triumphing over death.

熠熠之躯
Scintillating Flesh

由于金是一种永葆光泽的金属，埃及众神的躯体被认为是用黄金做成的。为木乃伊面具、棺木甚至逝者的皮肤加上金箔，可以令逝者的外形更接近神祇。逝者获得神的肉体，才更有可能获得永生，更有资格在来世与其他神祇同列。

黄金的熠熠生辉也象征着太阳的反射光，逝者为得永生，也希望得到太阳的照耀。用黄金制成的物件覆盖身体的行为也被认为能提供神奇的保护。因此，对于能负担得起这种仪式的极少数人来说，镀金装饰物是让他们从"暂时"的肉体向永生的神灵转变的一个重要因素。

As an untarnishable metal, gold was believed to be the substance from which the flesh of the Egyptian gods was made. Adding gold leaf to the mummy mask, coffin or even the skin of the deceased, made them more closely resemble a divinity. Attaining divine flesh better equipped the deceased for eternity and made them more deserving of joining the other gods in the afterlife.

Gold's glittering quality symbolized the reflection of the sun's rays, which the deceased hoped to enjoy for eternity. Even the act of covering an object in gold was thought to provide magical protection. Therefore, for the tiny minority who could afford it, gilded decoration was an important element in their transformation from temporary flesh to divine immortality.

"太阳神会为你的身体镀金，甚至给你的四肢镀上美丽的颜色。他会让你的肌肤金光闪闪"

——防腐仪式, 公元 1 世纪

"The sun god will gild your body for you, a beautiful colour even to the extremities of your limbs. He will make your skin flourish with gold"

The Embalming Ritual, 1st century AD

"镀金木乃伊的歪风邪气还在继续……这些可怜的人，脸上镀金，头上绘彩"

考古学家威廉 · 马修 · 弗林德斯 · 皮特里, 1888 年

"The plague of gilt mummies continues... wretched things with gilt faces and painted head pieces"

William Matthew Flinders Petrie, archaeologist, 1888

64

伊索斯女性木乃伊
Mummy of a Woman Called Isaious

约公元 1 世纪

镀金石膏、亚麻布和人体遗骸

高 188 厘米, 宽 58 厘米, 厚 39 厘米

埃及, 哈瓦拉

曼彻斯特博物馆藏

　　从这具木乃伊的镀金面具上可以看出逝者有着罗马风格的发型和首饰, 但是外面的裹尸布上却绘有埃及神祇的图样和象形文字。这位女性的名字用希腊语写在面具的顶部:"德米特里奥斯的女儿伊索斯"。面具上所体现的对来世的期望体现了多元文化的融合, 是公元 1 世纪哈瓦拉地区的典型特征。

C. 1st century AD

Gilded plaster, linen and human remains

Height 188 cm, Width 58 cm, Depth 39 cm

Egypt, Hawara

Manchester Museum

The gilded mask of this mummy shows the deceased with a Roman hairstyle and jewellery, but the outer shroud carries scenes of Egyptian gods and hieroglyphs. The name of the woman is written in Greek at the top of the mask: 'Isaious (or Isarous) daughter of Demetrios' (Ἰσαιοῦς Δημη[τρίου]). These multicultural expectations of the afterlife are typical of 1st century AD Hawara.

65

女性木乃伊
Mummy of a Woman

约公元 1 世纪
镀金石膏、亚麻布和人体遗骸
高 210 厘米, 宽 62 厘米, 厚 42 厘米
埃及, 哈瓦拉
曼彻斯特博物馆藏

　　这位无名女性有着时尚的罗马风格发型，佩戴着公元 1 世纪哈瓦拉地区典型的法老时期风格的螺旋蛇形手镯。尽管外裹尸布没有任何装饰过的痕迹，但她的面具却是用镀金石膏精心制作，并镶嵌着青铜制成的眼睛和睫毛。

C. 1st century AD
Gilded plaster, linen and human remains
Height 210 cm, Width 62 cm, Depth 42 cm
Egypt, Hawara
Manchester Museum

This unnamed woman has her hair in fashionable Roman style and wears Pharaonic-inspired coiled serpent bangles typical of 1st century AD Hawara. Although lacking any remaining trace of a decorated outer shroud, the mask is carefully modelled in gilded plaster with inlaid eyes and eyelashes added in bronze.

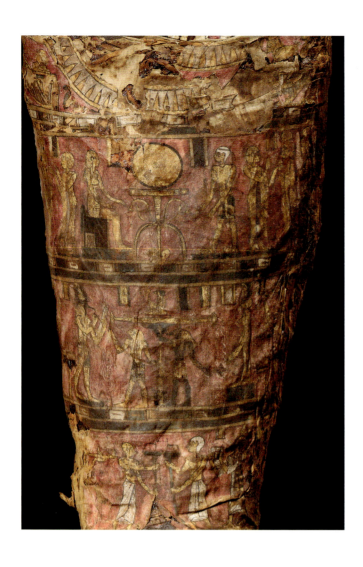

66

女孩木乃伊
Mummy of a Girl

约公元 1 世纪
镀金石膏、亚麻布和人体遗骸
高 110 厘米, 宽 40 厘米, 厚 43 厘米
埃及, 哈瓦拉
曼彻斯特博物馆藏

　　这位年轻女孩的木乃伊是成年女性木乃伊的缩小版, 她看起来像富有的罗马人, 面具为镀金混凝纸浆材质, 外裹尸布上绘有大量埃及图像——这是公元 1 世纪哈瓦拉地区木乃伊的典型特征。考古学家弗林德斯·皮特里在谈到她的首饰时, 相当傲慢地形容"太过华丽了"。

C. 1st century AD
Gilded plaster, linen and human remains
Height 110 cm, Width 40 cm, Depth 43 cm
Egypt, Hawara
Manchester Museum

Modelled in the form of an adult woman in miniature, this young girl appears both as a wealthy Roman in her gilded cartonnage mask and with extensive Egyptian scenes on her outer shroud. This is typical of 1st century AD Hawara. Remarking on her jewellery, the archaeologist Flinders Petrie described her rather haughtily as 'too splendaciously got up.'

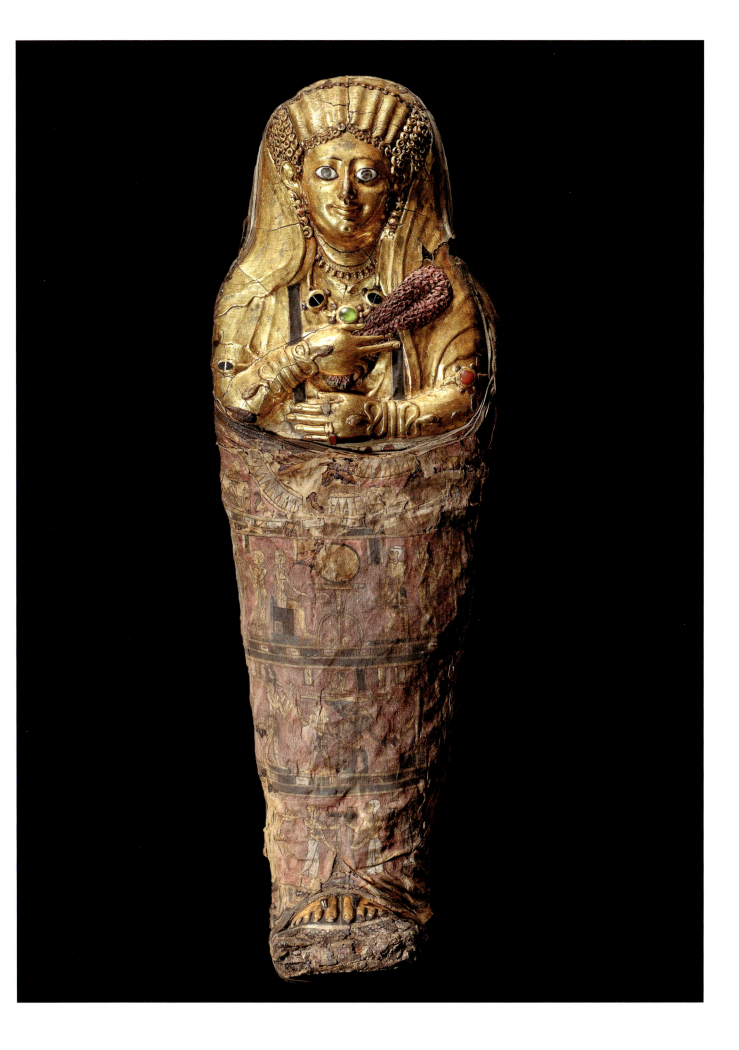

木乃伊面具
Mummy Mask

约公元 1 世纪

镀金和彩绘石膏

高 49.7 厘米, 宽 27.5 厘米, 厚 16 厘米

埃及, 哈瓦拉

曼彻斯特博物馆藏

　　传统的法老时期的木乃伊面具佩戴长长的头饰，现代人通常分辨不出性别的差异。这件不明身份的面具上卷曲的头发和耳环表明它来自一具女性木乃伊。

C. 1st century AD

Gilded and painted plaster

Height 49.7 cm, Width 27.5 cm, Depth 16 cm

Egypt, Hawara

Manchester Museum

With their long full headdresses, traditional Pharaonic mummy masks often appear rather genderless to a modern viewer. Both the stylized curls of hair and the presence of earrings indicate that this unidentified mask was intended for a woman.

木乃伊面具
Mummy Mask

约公元前 1 世纪

镀金和彩绘石膏

高 35 厘米, 宽 22 厘米, 厚 25 厘米

埃及, 发现地点未知

曼彻斯特博物馆藏

　　这副木乃伊面具的特征源于更早期的棺木和面具, 那一时期的面具会用带子绑住逝者的假胡须或者项链。肌肤区域的镀金是用长方形的金箔片贴成的。

C. 1st century BC

Gilded and painted plaster

Height 35 cm, Width 22 cm, Depth 25 cm

Egypt, findspot unknown

Manchester Museum

This mummy mask has a feature derived from much earlier coffins and masks, which may either show the straps used to attach a false beard or part of a necklace worn by the deceased. Patches of gilding have been applied in rectangles to the flesh areas.

木乃伊面具
Mummy Mask

约公元前 1 世纪
镀金和彩绘石膏
高 43.5 厘米, 宽 22.5 厘米, 厚 17 厘米
埃及, 哈赫温
曼彻斯特博物馆藏

  虽然闪闪发光的金色皮肤可以让逝者接近神祇, 但护身符可以提供更多的保护。将"瓦吉特之眼"即"荷鲁斯之眼"戴在额头上, 保护作用尤其显著, 所以我们可以看到有些"瓦吉特之眼"护身符被放在木乃伊前额上。

C. 1st century BC
Gilded and painted plaster
Height 43.5 cm, Width 22.5 cm, Depth 17 cm
Egypt, Lahun
Manchester Museum

While glittering golden skin identified the deceased as divine, additional protection might be provided by amuletic symbols. The wedjat eye – or 'Eye of Horus' – was especially protective when worn on the brow, and separate wedjat eye amulets have been found placed directly upon the forehead of mummies.

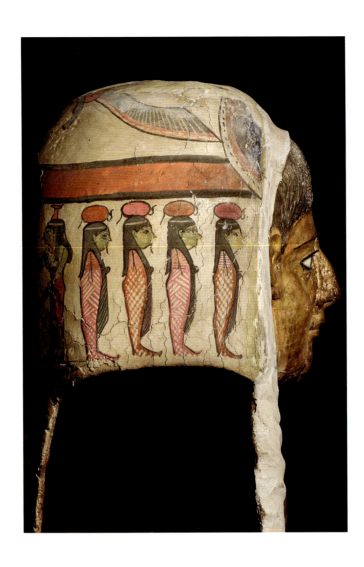

约公元 1 世纪

镀金和彩绘石膏

高 64 厘米, 宽 35 厘米

埃及, 哈瓦拉

曼彻斯特博物馆藏

70

男性木乃伊面具
Mummy Mask for a Man

　　这副精心制作的木乃伊面具画了一个留着山羊胡须的男人, 胡须不多, 他的脸仿佛是从一个兜帽里露出来的一样。他手持花环和一卷莎草纸——这是识字能力、知识和地位的象征。这副面具在现代被数次大面积修复过。

C. 1st century AD

Gilded and painted plaster

Height 64 cm, Width 35 cm

Egypt, Hawara

Manchester Museum

This elaborate mummy mask shows a man with a slight goatee style beard, emerging as if from a hood. He holds a floral wreath and a rolled-up papyrus – a sign of literacy, initiation and status. The mask has been extensively restored in modern times.

身份艺术
The Art of Identity

IV

　　罗马时期的木乃伊画像——即所谓的"法尤姆肖像"——是古代世界最引人注目的图像之一。他们在 19 世纪 80 年代被发现，改变了人们对艺术发展的看法。尽管这类木乃伊彩绘画像在埃及各地都有发现，但来自法尤姆地区的尤其多。每幅肖像都是用热蜡和颜料混合，在一块薄木板上绘制而成的，呈现出符合现代品味的逼真效果。

　　这种肖像画技法很可能起源于古代的意大利。和早期的木乃伊面具一样，木乃伊彩绘画像最初被用于覆盖在逝者的脸上，为逝者提供一幅永恒的（但可能是理想化的）面容。木乃伊画像上很少会写上逝者的名字，我们不知道被描绘的人的模样是否真的像他们的肖像中那样，甚至不知道他们是否是在离世前被描绘的。尽管现代人试图以年龄、种族或阶级来描述他们，但这些面孔的主人却仍然无法被归类。

Roman Period painted mummy panels – the so-called 'Faiyum Portraits' – are among the most striking images from the Ancient World. Their discovery in the 1880s changed what people had thought about the development of art. Although the portraits have been found at sites all over Egypt, examples from the Faiyum region are especially numerous. Each image was built up on a thin wooden panel using a mixture of hot wax and pigment, creating a life-like effect that appeals to modern tastes.

This technique of portrait painting likely originated in ancient Italy. Like earlier mummy masks, portrait panels were originally attached to cover the face of the deceased, to provide an eternal – but probably idealized – face for the deceased. Portrait mummies were rarely identified by name and we cannot know if the people portrayed actually looked as they do in their portraits, or even if they were painted before death. Despite modern attempts to characterize them in terms of age, race or class, these faces resist categorization.

哈瓦拉
Hawara

哈瓦拉遗址是与古埃及法老阿蒙涅姆赫特三世（约公元前 1831 年～公元前 1786 年）息息相关的的圣地。阿蒙涅姆赫特三世在哈瓦拉修建了一组恢弘的金字塔群，他去世后被埃及人奉为神明供于其中。由于希腊和罗马的访客将这个建筑群与希腊神话中克里特岛的迷宫联系在一起，使遗址名气大增。在"希腊 - 罗马"时期，法尤姆地区的人都希望自己能够埋葬在法老的金字塔附近。

英国考古学家威廉 · 马修 · 弗林德斯 · 皮特里（1853～1942 年）于 1888～1889 年和 1910～1911 年间雇用了 100 多名埃及工人，并主持了遗址的发掘工作。他的考古队发现了大量文物，包括数以万计的木乃伊，但他只记录了极小一部分饰以金绘或彩绘的木乃伊。

The site of Hawara was a sacred area associated with an ancient king, Amenemhat III (c. 1831–1786 BC). Amenemhat built an impressive pyramid complex at Hawara in which he was worshipped as a god after his death. Greek and Roman visitors identified this complex with a legendary structure called the Labyrinth, which added to the site's fame. During the Graeco-Roman Period, people from across the Faiyum region wanted to be buried near the king's pyramid.

William Matthew Flinders Petrie (1853–1942) was a British archaeologist who directed excavations at the site 1888–89 and 1910–11, typically employing over 100 Egyptian workmen. His teams discovered a huge range of objects, including the mummified remains of tens of thousands of bodies, but he only attempted to record the tiny percentage with golden or painted decoration.

" 通过头骨可以推断，这具木乃伊生前年轻貌美、五官精致、轮廓分明，是典型的希腊人 "

阿奇博尔德 · 萨伊斯, 考古学家, 1889 年

"The skull of the mummy showed that its possessor had been young and attractive looking, with features at once small, intellectual and finely chiselled, and belonging distinctively to the Greek type"

Archibald Sayce, archaeologist, 1889

"她的五官明显符合埃及人的特征……脸部表情透露出东方的慵懒"

阿米莉亚 · 爱德华兹, 小说家和埃及爱好者, 1891 年

"Her features are moulded in the unmistakable Egyptian type... the whole expression is of Oriental languor"

Amelia B. Edwards, novelist and Egyptophile, 1891

71

双面画像
Double-sided Portrait

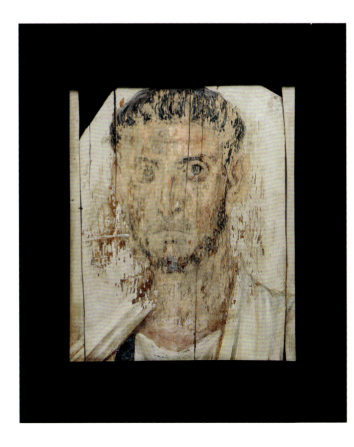

公元 2 世纪

彩绘木制

高 41 厘米, 宽 32.5 厘米

埃及, 哈瓦拉

曼彻斯特博物馆藏

　　这块木板的一面是一名年轻男子的画像, 他留着哈德良大帝统治时期 (罗马皇帝, 公元 117-138 年) 的流行发式。另一面则是一幅比较粗糙且部分图案已被抹去的草图, 因此完整的画像可能是为同一人所绘的更成熟的画像。

2nd century AD

Painted wood

Height 41 cm, Width 32.5 cm

Egypt, Hawara

Manchester Museum

On one side of this panel is an image of a youthful man with a hairstyle fashionable during the reign of the Emperor Hadrian (AD 117–138). On the reverse there is a rougher partially erased sketch, which perhaps represents a more mature version of the same man.

72

男子画像
Portrait of a Man

公元 2 世纪
彩绘木制
高 29.3 厘米, 宽 20 厘米
埃及, 哈瓦拉
曼彻斯特博物馆藏

　　男子露出的胸部象征了年轻与健壮, 体育场是贵族阶层重要的社交中心, 在体育场锻炼是罗马时代的埃及富人的消遣。画中男子的发型和胡须表明, 他生活的年代在罗马皇帝图拉真统治晚期或哈德良统治早期（公元 110-120 年）。

2nd century AD
Painted wood
Height 29.3 cm, Width 20 cm
Egypt, Hawara
Manchester Museum

This man's bare chest is a reference to athletic youthfulness, since exercising in the gymnasium – an important social hub for the elite – was a pastime of wealthy men in Roman Egypt. The subject's hairstyle and beard suggest a date late in the reign of the Emperor Trajan or early in that of Hadrian (AD 110 to 120).

公元 2 世纪

镀金石膏、亚麻布和人体遗骸

高 186 厘米, 宽 56 厘米, 厚 44 厘米

埃及, 哈瓦拉

曼彻斯特博物馆藏

　　这具来自哈瓦拉的男性木乃伊的画像上展示出一名蓄须的成熟男子形象。画像的绘画风格属于哈德良大帝统治时期（公元 117～138 年）。木乃伊外层的裹尸布上还绘有精致的圆领和传统的埃及葬礼场景。

2nd century AD

Gilded plaster, linen and human remains

Height 186 cm, Width 56 cm, Depth 44 cm

Egypt, Hawara

Manchester Museum

This mummy of a man from Hawara has a portrait showing a mature, bearded individual. The style of the portrait indicates a date during the reign of the Emperor Hadrian (AD 117–138). The outer wrappings carry a depiction of an elaborate collar and traditional Egyptian funerary scenes.

75

男性木乃伊
Mummy of a Man

约公元 1 ～ 2 世纪

镀金石膏、亚麻布和人体遗骸

高 186 厘米, 宽 54 厘米, 厚 40 厘米

埃及, 哈瓦拉

曼彻斯特博物馆藏

　　这具来自哈瓦拉的木乃伊是这一时期仅存的百余具木乃伊与画像均完好无损的木乃伊之一。画中的年轻人戴着月桂叶冠——这是死后得到宽恕的象征。CT 扫描显示, 这具木乃伊的身体有赘肉, 说明其生前体态丰腴, 这意味着画像很可能与其生前的相貌存在很大差异。

C. 1st-2nd century AD

Gilded plaster, linen and human remains

Height 186 cm, Width 54 cm, Depth 40 cm

Egypt, Hawara

Manchester Museum

This mummy from Hawara is one of only around 100 from this period which survive with the portrait intact. The portrait depicts a young man, wearing a crown of laurel leaves – a sign of justification after death. CT scans show folds of flesh which indicate obesity in life, meaning that the portrait is likely to differ significantly from his living appearance.

74

年轻男性木乃伊
Mummy of a Young Man

约公元 1 世纪
彩绘木制
高 35.5 厘米, 宽 17.5 厘米
埃及, 哈瓦拉
曼彻斯特博物馆藏

　　这名年轻男子身着一件被称为"克拉布斯"的、带有深红色条纹的白色束腰外衣, 左肩披着一件白色外衣。两件衣服都是身份的象征。男子的发型在弗拉维王朝（公元69 ～ 96 年) 十分流行。

75

年轻男子画像
Portrait of a Young Man

C.1st century AD
Painted wood
Height 35.5 cm, Width 17.5 cm
Egypt, Hawara
Manchester Museum

This young man wears a white tunic with a dark red stripe, called a 'clavus', and a white garment draped over his left shoulder – each a sign of status. The man's hairstyle was fashionable during the Flavian period (AD 69–96).

女子画像
Portrait of a Woman

约公元 2 世纪
彩绘木制
高 42.5 厘米, 宽 21.2 厘米
埃及, 哈瓦拉
曼彻斯特博物馆藏

　　这名女子身穿一件黑色金线镶边的紫色束腰外衣, 肩头裹着一件红色或浅紫色衣服。她的长发在头顶盘成一个高髻, 刘海中分。这种发型可以追溯到安东尼时代早期 (公元 138 ～ 160 年)。

C.2nd century AD
Painted wood
Height 42.5 cm, Width 21.2 cm
Egypt, Hawara
Manchester Museum

This woman wears a purple tunic bordered by a black band embroidered in gold. A red or light purple garment is wrapped around her shoulders. Her hair is coiled in a tall bun on top of her head and parted in the middle of her forehead. This hairstyle dates the portrait to the early Antonine period (AD 138–160).

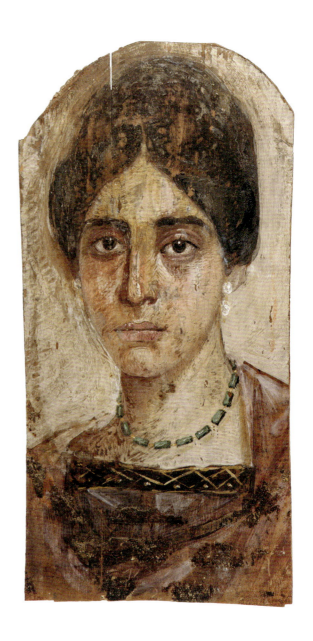

女子画像
Portrait of a Woman

约公元 2 世纪

彩绘木制

高 36.5 厘米, 宽 18 厘米

埃及, 哈瓦拉

曼彻斯特博物馆藏

　　这名女子的发型流行于哈德良大帝统治时期（公元 117 ～ 138 年）。女子身穿一件紫红色连衣裙，隐约可见浅绿色束腰外衣，佩戴的首饰包括一条深绿色宝石项链、一条珍珠项链和一对金镶珍珠耳饰。

C.2nd century AD

Painted wood

Height 36.5 cm, Width 18 cm

Egypt, Hawara

Manchester Museum

This woman's hairstyle dates the portrait to reign of the Emperor Hadrian (AD 117–138). The woman wears a purple-red dress with a light green under-tunic just visible. Her jewellery includes two necklaces, one of dark green stones, one of pearls and a pair of gold and pearl earrings.

78

年轻女子画像
Portrait of a Young Woman

约公元 2 世纪
彩绘木制
高 33 厘米, 宽 16.6 厘米
埃及, 哈瓦拉
曼彻斯特博物馆藏

　　画中人留着短发, 衣着难辨。有人认为这是一幅年轻男子的画像——但从脖颈处的一根编绳和一个吊坠判断, 这更像是一名女性。从她的发型可以看出, 这幅画像的创作年代可以追溯至公元 100 ～ 130 年。

C.2nd century AD
Painted wood
Height 33　cm, Width 16.6 cm
Egypt, Hawara
Manchester Museum

The person in this portrait has short hair and their clothing is difficult to discern. It has been suggested that this is a portrait of a young man. However, around the neck is a plaited cord and a pendant, which rather suggests a female. Her hairstyle indicates that the portrait dates to c. AD 100 to 130.

79

男子画像
Portrait of a Man

公元 1 世纪
彩绘木制
高 34.2 厘米, 宽 19.5 厘米
埃及, 哈瓦拉
曼彻斯特博物馆藏

　　这名男子穿着一件被称为"克拉布斯"的、带有深红色条纹的白色束腰外衣，左肩披着一件白色外衣。两件衣服都是身份的象征。男子的外貌表明，这幅画像绘于公元 1 世纪中期或晚期。

1st century AD
Painted wood
Height 34.2 cm, Width 19.5 cm
Egypt, Hawara
Manchester Museum

This man wears a white tunic with a dark red stripe, called a 'clavus', and a white garment draped over his left shoulder – each a sign of status. The appearance of the portrait suggests a date in the middle or late 1st century AD.

80

蓄须男子画像
Portrait of a Bearded Man

公元 2 世纪

彩绘木制

高 40.8 厘米, 宽 22.8 厘米

埃及, 哈瓦拉

曼彻斯特博物馆藏

　　画像中的男子身穿一件被称为"克拉布斯"的、前襟有一道深紫红色条纹的白色束腰外衣，左肩披着一件白色外衣。他有一头深色卷发，下颌下方的胡须修剪的很整齐。他的发型和着装风格表明，这幅画像的创作时间在公元 110 ~ 140 年间。

2nd century AD

Painted wood

Height 40.8 cm, Width 22.8 cm

Egypt, Hawara

Manchester Museum

This man wears a white tunic with a dark purple-red stripe, called a 'clavus', on the front. A white garment is draped over his left shoulder. The man has dark, curly hair and his beard is trimmed underneath his jawline. The style of his hair and clothing suggests a date of between AD 110 and 140.

81

女子画像
Portrait of a Woman

公元 2 世纪
彩绘木制
高 40 厘米, 宽 27 厘米
埃及, 哈瓦拉
曼彻斯特博物馆藏

　　画像中的女子穿着一件深红色束腰外衣, 戴着一对镶有珍珠的金耳环, 颈上还有一条圆形金珠与彩色宝石相间的项链。她的头发在头顶盘成一个大发髻, 刘海中分, 垂于脸部两侧。这种衣饰风格表明, 这幅画像的创作年代在公元138 ～ 160 年间的安东尼时代早期。

2nd century AD
Painted wood
Height 40 cm, Width 27 cm
Egypt, Hawara
Manchester Museum

This woman wears a dark red tunic, gold hoop earrings with pearls, and a necklace of coloured stones separated by round gold beads. Her hair is coiled in a large bun atop her head, with centrally parted waves around her face. This style dates the portrait to the early Antonine period, between AD 138 and 160.

82

女子画像
Portrait of a Woman

公元 1 ～ 2 世纪
彩绘木制
高 38 厘米, 宽 21 厘米
埃及, 哈瓦拉
曼彻斯特博物馆藏

　　画中女子穿着一件被称为"克拉布斯"的带有一道黑色条纹的紫红色束腰外衣，左肩披着一件紫红色衣服。几缕深色卷发垂在前额与耳前，其余则盘在头顶。这种发型表明，这幅画像的绘制时间在图拉真皇帝统治时期（公元 98 ～ 117 年）。

1st - 2nd century AD
Painted wood
Height 38 cm, Width 21 cm
Egypt, Hawara
Manchester Museum

This woman wears a reddish-purple tunic with a black stripe, called a 'clavus', and a reddish-purple garment drawn over her left shoulder. Her dark, curly hair is arranged in curls over her forehead and in front of her ears, with the rest of the hair on top of her head. This hairstyle suggests a date in the reign of the Emperor Trajan (AD 98–117).

83

蓄须男子画像
Portrait of a Bearded Man

公元 2 世纪
彩绘木制
高 45 厘米, 宽 29 厘米, 厚 3 厘米
埃及, 哈瓦拉
曼彻斯特博物馆藏

　　画中男子身穿一件带有暗红色条纹的白色束腰外衣
("克拉布斯"), 佩有一条镶钉剑带, 亦称"腰带"——
这是军装的标志, 表明该男子是一名士兵。他的发型和
胡须模仿了康茂德皇帝的第三种肖像类型, 从而可以确
定这幅画像绘于公元 185 ～ 195 年之间。

2nd century AD
Painted wood
Height 45 cm, Width 29 cm, Depth 3 cm
Egypt, Hawara
Manchester Museum

This man wears a white tunic with dark red stripes, called
'clavi', and a studded sword belt – or 'balteus'. These
indicate military dress and suggest that the man was a soldier.
His hairstyle and beard copy the third portrait type of the
Emperor Commodus, which dates this portrait to between
AD 185 and 195.

84

帕尔米拉的墓葬半身像
Funerary Bust From Palmyra

约公元 1 世纪
石灰岩
高 60 厘米, 宽 51 厘米
叙利亚, 帕尔米拉
曼彻斯特博物馆藏

C.1st century AD
Limestone
Height 60 cm, Width 51 cm
Syria, Palmyra
Manchester Museum

85

帕尔米拉的墓葬半身像
Funerary Bust From Palmyra

约公元 1 世纪

石灰岩

高 49 厘米, 宽 38 厘米

叙利亚, 帕尔米拉

曼彻斯特博物馆藏

C.1st century AD

Limestone

Height 49 cm, Width 38 cm

Syria, Palmyra

Manchester Museum

　　在木乃伊彩绘画像与面具流行于埃及的时代，罗马帝国的其他地方通过制作半身石像来纪念逝者。其中一座半身像表现的是一名包着头巾、绑着头带、戴着面纱的无名女子。另一座半身像雕刻的是一名手持书卷的蓄须男子。他的左边是用叙利亚帕尔米拉文字撰写的铭文："唉，雅亥，雅亥的儿子，哈拉普塔（之子）"。

Contemporary with mummy portraits and masks in Egypt, elsewhere in the Roman Empire stone busts were made to commemorate the deceased. One bust represents an unnamed woman wearing a veil over a turban and headband. The other depicts a bearded man who holds a book roll. To his left is an inscription in Palmyrene script: 'Alas, Yarhay, son of Yarhay, (son of) Halapta'.

遇见众神
Meeting the Gods

在埃及，大多数人都被禁止进入神庙，只能看到巨大外墙上的神像和象形文字。他们把神明做成小陶俑，以这种形式与神明"相遇"。比起埃及人，这些陶俑看起来更像希腊或罗马人。在人死后，古埃及诸神被召唤来帮助逝者，他们通常有着独特的动物头。豺狼头的阿努比斯神在罗马统治埃及的时代一直很受欢迎，他经常带着一把钥匙，帮助逝者进入来世。

虽然大部分人已经不认识古埃及象形文字，这种古老的文字仍会出现在贵族葬礼的装饰上，有时还会与精致的神像组合出现。古埃及人相信这些文字和图像有着神圣的力量，能确保逝者成功地过渡到来世。

Most people in Egypt were not allowed access to the sacred enclosures of the gods' temples and could only see the divine images and hieroglyphs on the monumental exterior walls. Everyday encounters with deities frequently took the form of small terracotta figurines in homes; these appear more Greek or Roman than Egyptian. However, after death ancient Egyptian gods – often with their distinctive animal heads – were invoked to help the deceased. Thus, the jackal-headed god Anubis remained popular into Roman times and is often shown with a key to help the deceased gain entry into the afterlife.

Even after Egyptian hieroglyphs ceased to be commonly understood, they appeared, along with sometimes elaborate images of the gods, on the funerary decorations of the wealthy. These were believed to envelop the deceased with magical, divine power to ensure a successful transition into the afterlife.

儿童木乃伊
Mummy of a Child

约公元 1 世纪

镀金石膏、亚麻布和人体遗骸

高 100 厘米, 宽 46 厘米, 厚 27 厘米

埃及, 哈瓦拉

曼彻斯特博物馆藏

这具木乃伊头部未被绷带覆盖的一小部分头饰上, 绘满了埃及诸神的保护图案, 面具受损部分下堆叠的亚麻布和石膏层展现了木乃伊棺的制作技术, 这件木乃伊的制作年代可以追溯到公元 1 世纪。

C.1st century AD

Gilded plaster, linen and human remains

Height 100 cm, Width 46 cm, Depth 27 cm

Egypt, Hawara

Manchester Museum

The small area of the headdress not covered by the bandages is filled with protective scenes of the Egyptian gods. The damaged area of the mask shows the cartonnage construction technique, built up in layers of linen and plaster, and dates to the 1st century AD.

女性木乃伊盖板
Mummy Cover of a Woman

约公元 1 世纪
镀金和彩绘石膏
高 155 厘米, 宽 57 厘米, 厚 24 厘米
埃及, 哈里杰
曼彻斯特博物馆藏

　　这名女子精致的螺旋形卷发和花卉头饰突出了欢乐的气氛, 袒露的双乳强调了性对重生的重要性。女子身体周围绘有大量无名神像, 这些是古埃及信仰中的常见主题, 可以为逝者提供保护。

C. 1st century AD
Gilded and painted plaster
Height 155 cm, Width 57 cm, Depth 24 cm
Egypt, Kharga
Manchester Museum

The elaborate corkscrew curls and floral headpiece of this woman emphasise festivity, and the unusually exposed breasts highlight the importance of sexuality for rebirth. Around the body are a large number of images of unnamed gods, a common motif in religious compositions, which provide protection to the deceased.

88

珠宝
Jewellery

约公元 1 世纪
镀金玻璃
宽 11 厘米
埃及, 萨夫特罕纳
曼彻斯特博物馆藏

C. 1st century AD
Gilded glass
Width 11 cm
Egypt, Saft el-Henna
Manchester Museum

89

珠宝
Jewellery

约公元 1 世纪
玻璃
宽 7 厘米
埃及，发现地点未知
曼彻斯特博物馆藏

C. 1st century AD
Glass
Width 7 cm
Egypt, findspot unknown
Manchester Museum

90

珠宝
Jewellery

约公元 1 世纪
玻璃
高 1 厘米, 宽 35 厘米
埃及, 发现地点未知
曼彻斯特博物馆藏

C. 1st century AD
Glass
Height 1 cm, Width 35 cm
Egypt, findspot unknown
Manchester Museum

约公元 1 世纪
玻璃
长 145 厘米
埃及, 萨夫特罕纳
曼彻斯特博物馆藏

C. 1st century AD

Glass

Width 145 cm

Egypt, Saft el-Henna

Manchester Museum

91

珠宝
Jewellery

约公元 1 世纪

镀金玻璃

高 1 厘米, 宽 30 厘米

埃及, 巴达里

曼彻斯特博物馆藏

在"希腊 - 罗马"时期, 人们常用多色玻璃代替更有
价值的宝石来制作珠宝首饰。有时还会在玻璃外部涂上一
层薄薄的黄金, 以达到流光溢彩的效果。这一时期, 此类
珠宝很可能是女性佩戴的饰物。

92

珠宝
Jewellery

C. 1st century AD

Gilded glass

Height 1 cm, Width 30 cm

Egypt, Badari

Manchester Museum

Multi-coloured glass was commonly used in jewellery during
the Graeco-Roman Period in place of more valuable stones,
sometimes being coated with a thin layer of gold to give eye-
catching iridescence. At this Period such jewellery was most
probably worn by women.

约公元 1 世纪
银
高 1.4 厘米
埃及, 高卡博尔
曼彻斯特博物馆藏

93

耳饰
Earring

　　这只简单的耳饰上有三个小球体, 很可能是女性饰物。在埃及, 白银并不常见, 因此这件耳饰显得不同寻常。

C. 1st century AD
Silver
Height 1.4 cm
Egypt, Qaw el-Kabir
Manchester Museum

Decorated with three small orbs, this simple earring was likely worn by a woman. Silver was less common than gold in Egypt, and so would appear more unusual.

94

一对耳饰
Pair of Earrings

约公元前 1 世纪
黄金
高 6.6 厘米
埃及，孟斐斯
曼彻斯特博物馆藏

　　这对精巧的耳饰是为贵族女性设计的，饰有非常精致的颗粒状饰物，在设计上与埃及风格大相径庭。

C. 1st century BC
Gold
Height 6.6 cm
Egypt, Memphis
Manchester Museum

These elaborate earrings for an elite woman are very delicately decorated with granulated work and appear rather un-Egyptian in design.

约公元 1 世纪

铜合金

高 9.2 厘米, 宽 5.7 厘米

发现地点未知

曼彻斯特博物馆藏

盘绕的蛇是权力和保护的象征, 它所具有的危险性可以战胜邪恶。"希腊 - 罗马"时期, 非皇室成员的墓葬习俗也采用了这种埃及皇室特权, 上层阶级女性的木乃伊盖板上也绘有类似的手镯纹样。

95

蛇形手镯
Snake Bracelet

C. 1st century AD

Copper alloy

Height 9.2 cm, Width 5.7cm

Findspot unknown

Manchester Museum

The coiled serpent was a symbol of power and protection, its dangerous aspect being harnessed to overcome evil. Such royal prerogatives were adopted in Graeco-Roman funerary customs of non-royal people and similar bangles are depicted on mummy mask coverings of elite women.

遗体保护
Preserving the Body

Ⅲ

  举行木乃伊制作仪式的目的不仅仅是为了保存遗体，而是为了创造一个完美、永恒"版本"的逝者，让他们的外表变得更接近神明。这样，灵魂就有了一个永久的"住所"，便于享受来世。

  制作木乃伊的过程复杂且昂贵，只有最富有的阶层才能享有完整的仪式过程。必要的材料包括泡碱（一种用于净化和干燥身体的、主要化学成分为碳酸钠的天然矿物），让身体散发芳香的植物树脂，以及用于包裹身体的大量亚麻布（主要目的是让尸体恢复生机，就像包扎伤口那样）。净化、涂油、包裹的全部过程都是在神殿中的神像面前进行的；这些仪式由专人主持，以将仪式对象（一具人类遗体，或一尊木制雕像）转化为神一样的存在。

  通常认为，木乃伊制作技术在罗马时期已经衰落，人们逐渐更注重木乃伊的外部装饰。但这是现代人的判断，并不能反映古人的初衷。木乃伊制作一直是一种神圣且秘而不宣的艺术。如今，像 CT 扫描和 X 光这样的无创分析使我们可以一窥木乃伊包裹下的秘密。

The aim of the ritual of mummification was not simply to preserve the body; it was to create a perfect, everlasting version of the deceased, one that resembled the form of an Egyptian god. In this way, the spirit would have a permanent physical home in order to enjoy the afterlife.

Creating a mummy was an elaborate and costly process and was only fully performed for the wealthiest people. Necessary materials included natron (a sodium chloride compound to purify and dry the body), plant resins to make the body fragrant, and large quantities of linen fabric to wrap the body (healing the corpse back to life, like a bandage round a wound). All of these processes – purification, anointing, wrapping – were also performed in temples on statues of gods; they were conducted by specialists in order to ritually transform something (a human corpse, a wooden statue) into a god-like being.

Mummification techniques are often said to have declined during the Roman Period, with focus shifting to the outer decoration of the mummy. This is more a modern judgement than a reflection of ancient intentions. Mummification was always a sacred and secret art. Today, non-invasive analysis like CT scans and X-rays provide an insight beneath the wrappings that we were never supposed to gain.

木乃伊的内部
Seeing Inside

　　许多人都痴迷于揭开木乃伊的裹尸布，看看里面究竟藏着什么。自古以来，盗墓者常常会为了寻找贵重的珠宝和护身符而扯碎这些裹尸布。公元 17 世纪，人们为了得到一种叫做"木米亚"的黑色物质而扒下木乃伊上的绷带，据说这种物质可以治疗疾病。在现代，好奇的研究人员则以"科学"的名义打开木乃伊的包裹。我们现在常以现代人的观点来描述古代人的健康问题。然而，这与埃及贵族死者努力追求的目标——完美且像神明一样不朽——形成了鲜明对比。

Many of us are fascinated by the unwrapping of mummies, to see what lies beneath the wrappings. Since ancient times, mummies were torn apart by tomb robbers in search of valuable jewellery and amulets. In the AD 1600s mummies were similarly stripped to provide a black substance called *mumia* believed to cure ailments. In modern times, curious investigators have unwrapped mummies in the name of 'science.' As a result, we now often describe ancient individuals in terms of what we perceive to be their health problems. This is, however, quite in contrast to the identity the elite Egyptian deceased strove for: to take on a perfect, god-like form for eternity.

" 没有哪个孩子生来就对木乃伊的制作过程感兴趣；成年人，
主要是教师，为他们提供了这些信息 "

伯纳德 · 博斯默, 埃及学家, 1976 年

"No child is born with a natural interest in mummification; adults,
primarily teachers, are their informants"

Bernard Bothmer, Egyptologist, 1976

约公元 1 世纪

费昂斯（主要成分为石英）

高 22 厘米，宽 19 厘米

埃及，（可能是）孟斐斯，1900 年捐赠

曼彻斯特博物馆藏

　　类似这种形状和材料的容器被用来盛放火化后的骨灰，这在希腊和罗马人中很常见。但在古埃及文化中，焚烧尸体的想法是难以置信的。火葬在埃及一直非常罕见。

骨灰瓮
Cinerary Urn

C. 1st century AD

Faience

Height 22 cm, Width 19 cm

Egypt, Likely from Memphis, Donation 1900

Manchester Museum

Vessels of similar shape and material were used to hold the ashes from cremations, which was practiced amongst the Greeks and Romans. The idea of burning the corpse was totally unthinkable to ancient Egyptian culture, and this method was never common in Egypt.

97

木乃伊眼罩
Eye Covers for a Mummy

约公元 1 世纪
黄金
高 2 厘米, 宽 1.2 厘米
埃及, 发现地点未知
曼彻斯特博物馆藏

　　"希腊 - 罗马"时期, 人们有时会直接将金片贴在木乃伊的身体上, 眼睛和舌头尤为重要, 需要特别保护。黄金是神灵身体的颜色, 用黄金制成的眼罩可以赋予逝者神性。

C. 1st century AD
Gold
Height 2 cm, Width 1.2 cm
Egypt, findspot unknown
Manchester Museum

Graeco-Roman Period mummies sometimes have pieces of gold applied directly to the body, with the eyes and the tongue being particularly important and in need of protection. Gold was associated with the flesh of the gods, and imparted divinity to the deceased.

约公元 2 世纪

木质

高 5 厘米, 宽 15 厘米, 厚 0.5 厘米

埃及, 发现地点未知

曼彻斯特博物馆藏

木乃伊标签
Mummy Label

　　由于许多"希腊 - 罗马"时期的木乃伊都没有姓名标识, 因此木乃伊上往往贴着写有逝者姓名的标签。这个木乃伊标签上以通俗埃及文和希腊文写着, 逝者名为塔塞尼森努特 (塞内松特), 并附有祈祷词: "愿她的巴灵活在奥西里斯 - 索卡尔面前, 阿拜多斯神……"

C. 2nd century AD

Wood

Height 5 cm, Width 15 cm, Depth 0.5 cm

Egypt, findspot unknown

Manchester Museum

As many Graeco-Roman mummies were not otherwise identified by name, they often had a mummy label attached naming the deceased. This example carries text in both Demotic Egyptian and Greek, giving the name of the deceased as Tasenetsenut (Senesonthis), along with the prayer: 'May her Ba-spirit live before Osiris-Sokar, lord of Abydos...'

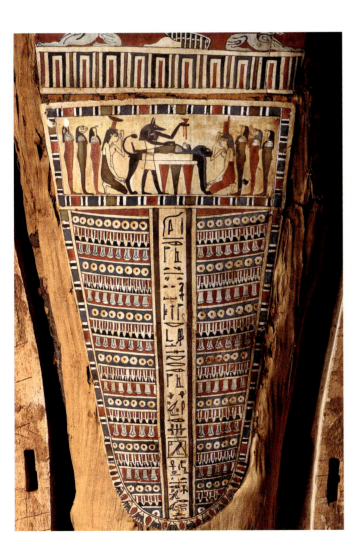

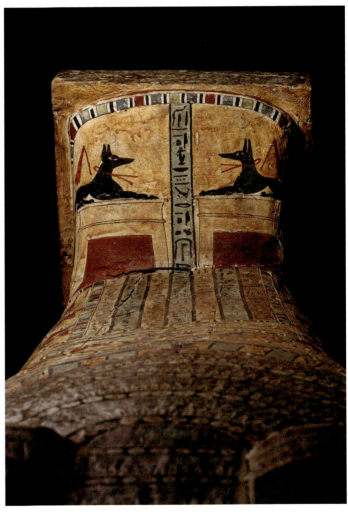

现代阐释
Reception

VIII

现在陈列在世界各地博物馆里成千上万的埃及文物并不是碰巧散落各处的。考古学家、工人、收藏家和赞助人都在文物流转的过程中发挥了作用。

英国对埃及的殖民统治——特别是在 1882 年至 20 世纪 20 年代间——使西方考古学家得以对一些遗址进行发掘，并向埃及政府索取他们发现的文物。在西方，从国家博物馆到个人爱好者都想拥有古埃及文物，这推动了发掘、收藏和研究诠释产业的发展。

埃及古物学家弗林德斯·皮特里爵士对他发现的木乃伊"种族"非常感兴趣，他分析了法尤姆肖像主人的外貌，并收集和测量了木乃伊的头骨，试图对此进行调查研究。皮特里得出结论，这些木乃伊大多数是在埃及的希腊定居者，虽然我们现在认为，居住在哈瓦拉的精英人群要混杂得多。基于西方对埃及木乃伊和不朽神话的迷恋，当时新发现的法尤姆肖像的展览甚至激发了奥斯卡·王尔德的灵感，写下了小说《道林·格雷的画像》。

The many thousands of Egyptian antiquities now in museums around the world did not arrive by chance. Archaeologists, workmen, collectors and patrons all played their part. British colonial control of Egypt – especially between 1882 and the 1920s – enabled Western archaeologists to excavate at sites and to claim a share of their finds from the Egyptian government. In the West, collectors – from national museums to individual hobbyists – wanted to own a piece of ancient Egypt, and drove the industry of excavation, acquisition and interpretation.

Egyptologist, Sir Flinders Petrie was very interested in the 'race' of the mummies he found, interpreting the appearance of the Faiyum portraits and collecting and measuring the skulls of mummies to try to investigate this. He concluded that most were Greek settlers in Egypt, although we now believe the elite population of Hawara was much more mixed. Building on Western fascination with Egyptian mummies and immortality, the display of the newly-discovered Faiyum portraits even inspired Oscar Wilde to write his novel *The Picture of Dorian Gray*.

商人与爵士
Merchant Princes

与美国和欧洲许多城市的博物馆一样，曼彻斯特博物馆也是蓬勃发展的工业的受益者。杰西 · 霍沃斯（1835～1920年）是一位富有的棉花实业家。美国南北战争结束后，作为"制棉中心"的曼彻斯特摆脱了对美国南部原棉的依赖，转而向以棉花作为主要经济作物的埃及获取原料。

霍沃斯曾于1880年前往埃及旅行，此后便迷上了那里，他对埃及与《圣经》之间的联系尤其感兴趣。霍沃斯资助了埃及考古学家皮特里的实地考察，并与他成了朋友。皮特里将获准带出埃及的文物中的三分之一送给了霍沃斯，霍沃斯随后将它们捐赠给了曼彻斯特博物馆。

Like many city museums in the US and Europe, Manchester Museum was funded by the profits of industry. Jesse Haworth (1835–1920) was a wealthy cotton industrialist. Following the American Civil War, the Egyptian economy of the later 19th century was dominated by growing cotton crops to provide much of the raw material processed by Manchester's many cotton mills.

Haworth became fascinated with Egypt after traveling there in 1880 and was especially interested in its connections to the Bible. He funded the fieldwork of archaeologist William Matthew Flinders Petrie, with whom he became friends. Haworth received one third of the finds that Petrie was allowed to take out of Egypt as part of the 'finds division' system, and subsequently donated these to Manchester Museum.

《千里尼罗河》
A Thousand Miles Up the Nile

约 1878 年
纸张和皮革
高 27 厘米, 宽 21 厘米, 厚 6.4 厘米
曼彻斯特博物馆藏

　　阿米莉亚 · 爱德华兹（1831 ～ 1892 年）是一位广
受欢迎的旅游作家与埃及爱好者。她走遍英国和美国，为
埃及探险基金筹集资金。杰西 · 霍沃斯和妻子在前往埃
及之前阅读了这本书，随后他们开始支持弗林德斯 · 皮
特里在埃及的发掘工作。本书是阿米莉亚赠给玛丽安 ·
霍沃斯的亲笔签名本。

C. 1878
Paper and leather
Height 27 cm, Width 21 cm, Depth 6.4 cm
Manchester Museum

Amelia B. Edwards (1831–1892) was a popular travel writer
and Egyptophile who toured the UK and US to raise money for
the Egypt Exploration Fund. Jesse Haworth and his wife read
this book before undertaking a trip to Egypt, and subsequently
supporting Flinders Petrie's excavations in Egypt. This copy is
autographed by Amelia to Marianne Haworth.

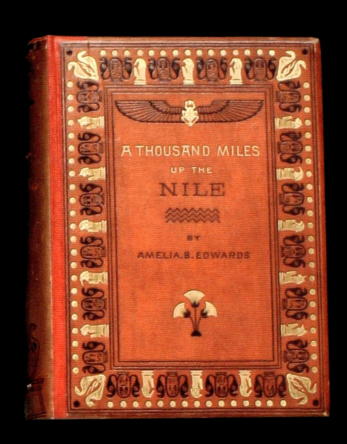

A THOUSAND MILES
UP THE
NILE

BY

AMELIA. B. EDWARDS

IOI

杰西 · 霍沃斯和玛丽安 · 霍沃斯的半身像
Busts of Jesse and Marianne Haworth

约 1915 年
大理石
高 36 厘米, 宽 40 厘米, 厚 25 厘米
曼彻斯特博物馆藏

　　杰西 · 霍沃斯（1835 ~ 1920 年）是曼彻斯特博物馆的主要资助人。他和妻子玛丽安曾于 1880 年访问埃及，此后便对埃及学产生了浓厚的兴趣。新教信仰或许是促使杰西 · 霍沃斯选择支持与圣经有关的考古学的原因。玛丽安 · 霍沃斯在丈夫去世后继续为博物馆提供支持。

C. 1915
Marble
Height 36 cm, Width 40 cm, Depth 25 cm
Manchester Museum

Manchester Museum's major financial benefactor was Jesse Haworth (1835–1920), who became fascinated with Egyptology after he and his wife Marianne visited Egypt in 1880. Haworth's non-conformist Christian beliefs may have inspired his wish to support archaeology with possible Biblical connections. Marianne Haworth continued to support the Museum after her husband's death.

被制成木乃伊后，逝者的"巴"（灵魂）  来到杜阿特（来世[区域]），与众神会面。知晓众神的名字，才能获得他们的帮助，并通过奥西里斯的审判，得到永生。

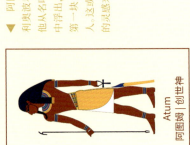

Atum 阿图姆|创世神

▼ 阿图姆是"全部之主"，赫利奥利斯神系的主神。据称他从名叫"努恩"的原始混沌池水中浮出，站在露出洋大海的第一块土丘上创造了万物和人。这或许是金字塔形状背后的灵感来源。

Tefnut 泰芙努特|湿气之神

▼ 常被表现为人身母狮子，埃及学家说她是水分的"温气"或"露湿性的带有水分的空气"。她有时会被称为太阳神拉的眼睛。

Shu 舒|空气之神

▼ 通常被表现为头上顶着一根羽毛的男子。在表现创世的画面上，可以看到舒站在他神盖布上面，用双手托起天神努特。

Nut 努特|天空之神

▼ 站立时，以头上的水罐作为标志。也常被表现为作天穹状的女子，用胳膊和腿把自己从大地上支撑起来，她的身体象征日月星辰运行的轨道。

Geb 盖布|大地之神

▼ 站立时，他是一个头上顶着鹅的男子；侧躺时，是一个绿色的男子（有时装点着植物）。在有关荷鲁斯和赛特争夺王位的神话故事里，盖布协助太阳神拉进行判决，传说中诸神为此进行审判的建筑物被称为"主神殿"或"盖布的大厅"。

通常呈一个木乃伊的形状，手上拿着法老使用的权杖和连枷，头戴阿太夫王冠。因为他是掌管冥界的神明，根据《亡灵书》的描述，通常要经过审判关。并接受奥西里斯的审判，才能重生。他的皮肤是绿色或者黑色的，象征植物和尼罗河的肥沃土地。

在奥西里斯神话里，伊希斯寻找被赛特谋杀的丈夫奥西里斯的尸体，使他复活，抚养儿子荷鲁斯长大成人，然后帮助他从赛特手里夺回被篡夺的王位。

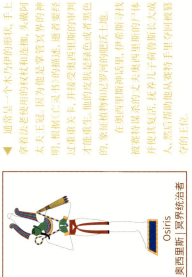
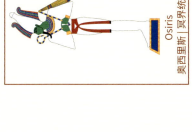

Osiris
奥西里斯｜冥界统治者

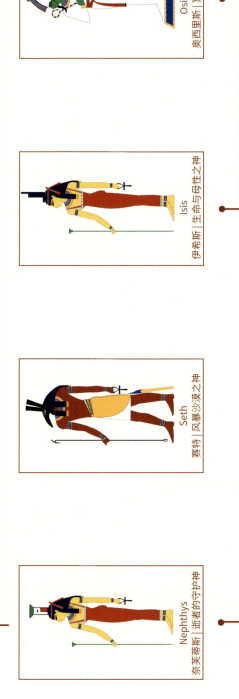

Isis
伊希斯｜生命与母性之神

Seth
赛特｜风暴沙漠之神

Nephthys
奈芙蒂斯｜逝者的守护神

爱与美的女神，人们把她与欢乐、音乐、舞蹈和酒精饮品联系起来。在希腊神奥波利斯神系里，他是荷鲁斯的配偶，他的名字在象形文字里有"荷鲁斯的庙"之意。

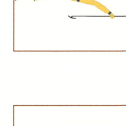

Hathor
哈托尔｜欢乐与爱情之神

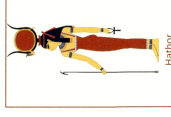

Horus
荷鲁斯｜王权之神

豺头狗形状或者长着豺狗的头、人身的神。相传他曾经把被谋杀的奥西里斯的尸体制作成木乃伊，使得后者的尸体得以保存并最终获得再生，因此他的主要职责是为逝者制作木乃伊，以及在来生审判仪式称量逝者的心脏。

Anubis
阿努比斯｜墓地保护神

人形的伊姆塞特，保护肝；狗头的杜阿木太夫，保护胃；豺猫头的哈皮，保护肺；鹰头的克伯塞努夫，保护肠。他们的形象常被制成盖子，装进各内脏器官。

Four sons of Horus
荷鲁斯四子

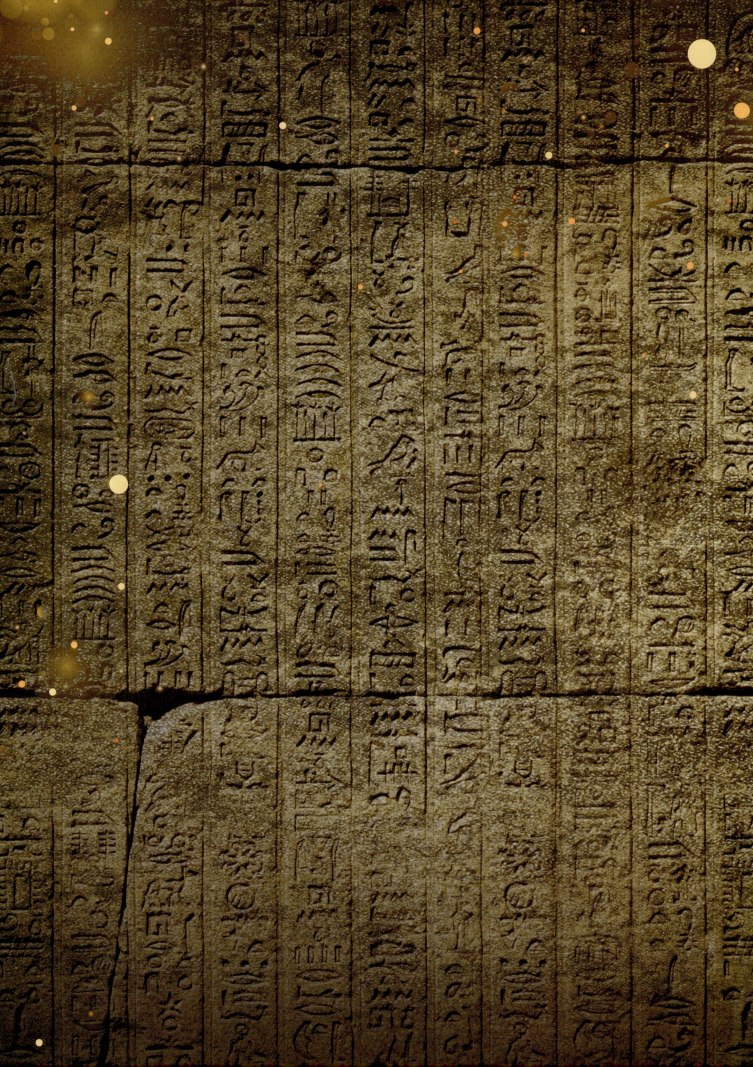